VEGAN MEAL PREP

Vegan MEAL PREP

READY-TO-GO MEALS and SNACKS for HEALTHY PLANT-BASED EATING

JL FIELDS

Photography by Darren Muir

ROCKRIDGE
PRESS

Always for the animals.

Interior and Cover Designer: William D. Mack
Editor: Stacy Wagner-Kinnear
Production Editor: Erum Khan
Photography by Darren Muir, © 2018, Food styling by Yolanda Muir

ISBN: Print 978-1-64152-290-8 | eBook 978-1-64152-291-5

R1

Contents

Introduction

If you picked up this book because you're new to meal prepping *and* new to vegan cooking, I've got great news: You're about to master both.

The heart of meal prep is bulk (or batch) cooking. Plant-based food groups—beans and legumes, grains, vegetables, fruit, and nuts and seeds—are perfect for advance preparation, from meals to snacks to dessert. The art of meal prep is to take those batch-cooked foods and turn them into portable, portion-controlled meals to reheat and eat throughout the week.

So, yes, "I'm too busy to cook" folks, this book is for you.

Actually, it's the book I wish I had eight years ago when I transitioned from vegetarian to vegan. Lucky me; up until that point, my husband did most of the cooking. But he felt a little lost when I announced my dietary decision, and suddenly I was in the kitchen for the first time in years trying to figure out cooking—and plant-based cooking at that.

It didn't take me long to discover that planning was everything. I began spending an hour or two in the kitchen on the weekend preparing a few beans and grains—two hearty plant-sourced staples—to reheat and eat with vegetables during the week. I had a few bumps along the way, though, because sometimes I got a little too ambitious and would end up making far more food than we could eat, and some of it would go to waste.

That's when meal prep saved the day (and the food). Instead of making huge batches of one food, I started creating recipes designed for a set number of meals per week. I portioned out those recipes, layering them in single-serving containers, to create the ultimate "fast food." Storing them in the refrigerator (and sometimes on the counter), I could see exactly what meals I had ready to eat, and I cut down on waste.

This advance cooking and prepping technique actually catapulted me into a culinary career. I morphed from enthusiastic home cook into a cookbook author, university culinary instructor, and cooking coach. I also prep meals for private clients on a weekly basis.

And now meal prep is hot, hot, hot in many kitchens. Most people are motivated to meal prep to eat healthier, avoid spending too much time in the kitchen, and have a little more control of portion sizes. While it may sound too good to be true, meal prepping can help you do all of this! It might feel

a little overwhelming at first, but I'll be right next to you, sharing what I've learned over the years, offering simple yet delicious recipes that are perfectly portioned for prep.

You'll find 70 recipes ideal for advance cooking and eight "preps" that coach you for the week, step by step. The preps will vary by type of meal. Have dinner meetings all week? Choose a breakfast and lunch prep and build your culinary muscles. More importantly, since many of you are new to vegan eating and cooking, you'll learn how to create balanced plant-based meals because the preps star beans, vegetables, grains, fruit, and nuts and seeds—all of the five vegan food groups!

Remember, this book is a guide, not a prescription, so don't get hung up on the notion that you need to make preps every week or that you have to follow them from prep one to eight. But do remember that during those excruciatingly busy weeks when you're not even sure you'll have a chance to catch your breath, you can give yourself the gift of time by carving out a few hours to create nourishing, healthy food that will sustain your energy through the most hectic of weeks.

Part One

VEGAN MADE EASY

PLANT-POWERED PREP

What exactly *is* meal prepping? It's the highest-level meal planning you can do: Prepare food, portion it out into single-serving meals, and store it. In this case, plants are the star of those perfectly-portioned preps. You'll be making vegan mains and sides and some one-pot meals that can be reheated, as well as simple salads that you can grab and eat right away.

You may already know that vegan foods are considered healthy for good reason: no cholesterol and lots of fiber! If gaining control of portion sizes, losing weight, and/or reversing or preventing disease are your motivations for eating plant-based meals—or you're simply ready to create healthy foods at home—having the structure of meal prepping should really help you along toward those goals.

« Miso Root Veggies (page 95)

Vegan for All

Plant-based eating is on the rise. That's likely why you picked up this book. Here are a few reasons why so many are transitioning to this way of eating.

Health: In my own practice, clients come to me after a doctor recommends a plant-based diet over medication for food-related health issues, like high cholesterol. Some choose a vegan diet due to lactose, milk, and egg allergies. And, of course, some are motivated to lose weight (and, as with any diet, your results may vary). Research additionally tells us that, on average, vegans have a lower BMI (body mass index), are less likely to have type 2 diabetes and hypertension, and are less likely to develop some cancers than people who do not follow a plant-based diet.

Environmental concerns: The farming of animals contributes more global greenhouse gas emissions than transportation, causing rising temperatures and sea levels. Livestock and their by-products account for at least 32 billion tons of carbon dioxide per year, or 51 percent of all worldwide greenhouse gas emissions. And while millions worldwide lack sufficient access to affordable, nutritious food, 35 percent of grains grown globally is fed to livestock.

Compassion: In 1944, the Vegan Society defined the vegan ethic as "a way of living which seeks to exclude, as far as is possible and practicable, all forms of exploitation of, and cruelty to, animals for food, clothing, or any other purpose." Many vegans, including me, chose this way of life for this simple reason: Why harm another being when we don't have to?

Whatever the motivation, eating a plant-sourced diet is good for the planet, for animals, and for YOU.

Meal Prep + Vegan = Healthier

Using whole, plant-based foods is the heart of healthy cooking and vegan meal prepping. Begin each week by taking a serious look at your schedule. Where do you need help? Early morning meetings may mean a breakfast prep or two will ensure you start each day off right. Long days may be the reason you need dinner preps all week long. Carving out an hour or two over the weekend or on a day off to prepare dried or canned beans, fast- or slower-cooking grains, and a variety of vegetables will set you up for success. You will:

- Combine mains, sides, and snacks that are portion-controlled.
- Feel fuller longer by filling up on nutrient-dense foods.
- Make wiser choices by opting for readily available home-cooked snacks versus packaged.

Meal Prep Benefits

Vegan meal prepping is a healthy choice, but don't forget some of the other amazing benefits.

Save time. Most of us want a delicious home-cooked meal morning, noon, and night, but it often feels like our schedule doesn't allow for it. Investing a few hours a week in meal prepping frees up your days for the remainder of the week. In the morning you can reheat a hearty bowl of oats or grab a smoothie on the way out the door. Ramp up your lunch with a satisfying salad filled with precooked beans and grains. And relax in the evening and spend some time with your family because dinner is ready—all you have to do is reheat it! Bonus: If you have an Instant Pot® or pressure cooker, I will provide tips throughout the book on how to adapt recipes for pressure cooking, which will save you even more time.

Save money. I don't know about you, but if I haven't planned ahead, I tend to overbuy at the grocery store. Meal prepping to the rescue! Mapping out recipes and meals for the week means you buy what you need. Period. And meal prepping often uses the same ingredients across various meals, so you save money by purchasing larger cans of beans and dry grains in bulk.

Build your plant-based culinary muscles. As you become a pro at meal prepping, you'll also learn and begin applying flavor profiles and texture variety to your meals. When I first went vegan, I found myself in a rut. I thought my diet was "just" beans, greens, and grains. Well, I was sort of right, except it's not "just"—it's so many of all three! I learned to repurpose foods with taste and texture. For instance, I would make a big batch of black

PROTEIN, GRAIN, AND GREEN COMBINATIONS

As I mentioned, to eat vegan, you only need to focus on the five plant-based food groups:

1. Vegetables
2. Fruit
3. Beans and legumes
4. Grains
5. Nuts and seeds

That's it! And those five food groups prep beautifully. Drizzle a delicious cashew- or almond-based cream sauce over a bowl of braised greens, spicy lentils, and brown rice cooked with dried cranberries, and you've got all of the five vegan food groups in one dish.

Of course, one of the most common questions I hear is "Where will I get my protein?" From my experience teaching classes and coaching clients over the years, I know that most times this question could be replaced with "What do I eat to replace the meat, cheese, or eggs?" You already know my answer: Plants! Some of the most protein-packed plants include:

Legumes and beans: These include lentils, chickpeas, and the full range of beans of all colors and types, not to mention peanuts.

Quinoa: Technically a seed, it's considered an "honorary legume."

Tofu and tempeh: These great vegan meat alternatives are made from 100 percent legumes.

Nuts: Choose from a wide variety of nuts, including pistachios, almonds, cashews, and more.

Cooking beans and grains is easy on the stove, easier with a slow cooker, and fast with a pressure cooker or Instant Pot. Roast root vegetables for 30 to 40 minutes and steam leafy greens with lemon juice, and you'll enjoy savory veggies all week. Toss nuts or seeds into a blender with a little vinegar, garlic, and water, and you'll have a creamy sauce in seconds. Keep fresh fruit in a bowl on the counter for quick snacks. See? You've got this!

The vegan meal prep key is to strengthen your spice game (this is what I mean by building your plant-based culinary muscles). As you begin and continue weekly meal prep, you'll see that you can take many recipe concepts and simply switch up an herb or spice or a simple ingredient and completely transform the flavor.

Here are some of my favorite ways to do just that:

BALANCED BASICS	FLAVOR KICK
Chickpeas + couscous + Swiss chard	South Asian spices, such as garam masala, cardamom, and cinnamon, offer a sweet heat.
White beans + polenta + arugula	Toss with lemon juice and fresh sage. Sprinkle finely chopped cashews and walnuts over the top for a quick, whole-food, nondairy Parmesan.
Diced potatoes + parsnips + quinoa	Balsamic vinegar and red pepper flakes add umami.
Bean chili + leafy greens	Stir raw spinach into the hot chili before adding pickled jalapeños (more umami!) and a dollop of plain vegan yogurt.
Chickpea salad + avocado + pita	Sprinkle on dulse (seaweed) flakes for a vegan version of a tuna salad sandwich.
Peppers stuffed with quinoa + black beans + corn	Mix in cilantro, lime, and spiced roasted pumpkin seeds (pepitas).
Cauliflower steaks + roasted Brussels sprouts	Finish with a dollop of chickpeas puréed with cumin and lemon juice.

beans over the weekend but avoid seasoning them. One night I would use them in a chili-style soup with red onion, chili powder, and cilantro. The next day for lunch, I would purée them with tahini and cumin for a black bean dip wrap. And the next morning, I would use them in a breakfast bowl by simply adding them to stir-fried vegetables, then spooning the beans and veggies over savory oats. Learning to switch up flavors and add interesting textures is a fun way to become a more interesting cook and satisfied plant eater.

Meal Prep Principles

Everyone is unique, and your weekly meal prep approach might be different from mine. And that's great because this is going to work best if you find the approach just right for you. How and how often you choose to meal prep is your choice. That said, I think you'll find that these principles will work for everyone.

START SIMPLE

You don't have to follow the eight preps in this book from 1 to 8. Start exactly where you need help today. If you're spending too much money going out for lunch, start with prep 4 (page 31) and you're set with lunch and snacks for five days. If you're too tired to cook after a long day of work, start with prep 5 (page 35), where you will have meals that can easily be used for lunch or dinner, provide simple seasonings that pack a flavorful punch, and are filled with hearty beans, grains, and vegetables.

SET REALISTIC GOALS

It's easy to think that from this day forward, you will meal prep every meal from now until the end of time. Maybe. Or maybe sometimes you will have to go with the flow and go with your schedule. Sit down with your calendar and look at your week. What meals would you like to quickly heat or grab and eat next week? Now decide which recipes you want to make. This is going to save you time, save you money, and help you avoid overprepping and wasting food.

New vegans often are overwhelmed by the variety of vegetables, grains, and bean choices. Consider this a (fun) challenge. As you plan for the week, pick a recipe that has a bean or grain you've never used before. You'll begin to discover your likes and dislikes, and you'll learn just how versatile these plant-powered foods really are. One day you can eat cooked beans as is, and the next day you can turn the leftovers into a bean dip. You can serve farro as a side with tofu and roasted vegetables for dinner and the next day reheat it with a little almond milk and maple syrup for a breakfast bowl or stir it into vegetable broth and a can of tomatoes for a quick soup for lunch.

Inspired Batch Cooking

In addition to the eight 1-week meal preps, this book is filled with recipes that are ideal for batch cooking. Take a recipe or two, cook them in bulk (double or even triple, if you like), and freeze for later. A few months down the road, during a week you can't meal prep, pull a jar of grains and a bag of beans out of the freezer, thaw, then reheat and eat with a simple salad or steamed vegetable.

My batch-cooking basics:

1. Cook a kind of bean, grain, or vegetable.

2. Drain any excess liquid.

3. Spread out on a sheet pan to cool.

4. Using a permanent marker, note the food and date on the label of a quart-size freezer-safe bag. Consider investing in ecofriendly reusable food storage bags; in this case, use a dry-erase marker on the bag for storage.

5. Using a measuring cup, portion a 1- or 2-cup serving into the bag (I like to note the quantity on the label).

6. Gently press the air out and seal.

7. Lay the bags flat in the freezer. To start, you can place all the bags on a sheet pan. Once frozen, remove from the pan and arrange in the freezer.

I tend to make grains and beans in bulk each weekend. I can take those foods and turn them into a variety of meals. For example:

- Simple supper: Reheat black beans and brown rice and serve over a steamed or stir-fried vegetable.
- Wrap sandwich: Purée black beans, spread on a tortilla, sprinkle with raw vegetables, and roll it up.
- Easy soup: Heat vegetable broth with two handfuls of leafy greens, a cup of cooked black beans, and a cup of cooked brown rice.
- Taco bowl: Reheat brown rice and black beans with a can of fire-roasted tomatoes and serve with chopped onion and cilantro.

Tasty meals in minutes, all because I did some batch cooking!

UMAMI

Throughout the book, I make a point to use very accessible ingredients. I note this for the seasoned vegan cook who may think, "Well, this isn't very challenging." You're right. This book is about getting good—seriously good—food together in a reasonable amount of time so you can eat all week. If you have additional steps or flavors you want to add, go for it! The simplicity is by design for newbies: those new to meal prepping and/or plant-based cooking.

And that brings me to "umami." New vegans and plant-based eaters, you may learn about some new ingredients: nutritional yeast and miso paste, for example. I want you to experiment and try (just a few) new things, particularly when it comes to ingredients you might not have used in your cooking before. I focus a good deal of my seasoning techniques and flavor profiles on umami, a concept in Japanese cooking often referred to as the "fifth flavor." Certain foods and cooking techniques bring out this savory essence, adding a mysterious "wow" to a dish. Such foods include ripe tomatoes, mushrooms (dried and fresh), fermented foods (such as sauerkraut, miso, and soy sauce), wine, nutritional yeast, and more. Cooking techniques that can yield umami include caramelizing and roasting—both of which are included in this book.

Go-To Ingredients

Vegan ingredients are ideal for batch cooking and meal preps. While you'll see all kinds of beans, vegetables, and whole grains, I do try to use similar ingredients frequently to save you money and allow you to use the ingredients a variety of ways. Beans and grains are going to store well in the refrigerator (up to 5 days) and do equally well in the freezer. Some vegetables store better than others in the freezer, and I'll always note storage tips in each recipe.

While there's a wide variety to choose from in the plant kingdom, I do have some favorites that can take on a variety of flavors simply by adjusting the spices. I'll recommend dried spices (affordable and often easy to purchase in bulk) over fresh most often, and I'll also recommend sauces and vinegars that add a real flavor punch without breaking the bank. And as much as I love fresh lemon and lime juice and fresh-pressed garlic, go ahead and pick up shelf-stable bottled lemon juice and a big jar of minced garlic. I do. Both keep well in the refrigerator, and you'll save money and time. And keep a variety of vegetable broth (boxed liquid, concentrate, bouillon cubes, and powder) on hand. I always have vegetable, no-chicken, and no-beef broth varieties in the cupboard.

Here are my ingredient staples:

VEGETABLES

- Carrots
- Celery
- Collard greens
- Mushrooms
- Onions
- Romaine lettuce
- Russet potatoes
- Spinach
- Sweet potatoes
- Tomatoes

PROTEINS

- Beans (pinto, white, black, and chickpeas)
- Lentils
- Nondairy milk
- Nondairy yogurt
- Peanuts
- Quinoa
- Tempeh
- Tofu

WHOLE GRAINS

- Brown rice
- Farro
- Oats
- Pasta
- Polenta
- Whole-wheat pitas
- Whole-wheat tortillas

FRUIT
- Bananas
- Berries
- Dried fruit

FATS (NUTS AND OILS)
- Almonds
- Cashews
- Nonstick cooking spray
- Olive oil
- Seeds
- Sesame oil
- Vegan butter

HERBS, SPICES, AND MORE
- Balsamic vinegar
- Basil, dried
- Chili powder
- Cinnamon, ground
- Cumin, ground
- Curry powder
- Lemon juice
- Minced garlic
- Oregano, dried
- Red pepper flakes
- Soy sauce or gluten-free tamari
- Vegetable broth
- Vegan Worcestershire sauce (I recommend Annie's, Edward & Sons, and Whole Foods' 365 brand)

WHAT NOT TO PREP

Good news: Most plant-based ingredients prep perfectly and freeze well, too. The exceptions include some leafy greens, roasted vegetables, and fruit, like avocado. That's why you'll see me using leafy greens like arugula in a soup or in a one-pot meal, because the tender texture does not freeze well.

Manage your expectations with reheated roasted vegetables; though still tasty, the texture varies and they may fare better when mixed into a soup with leftover beans or even wrapped up in a tortilla with bean dip. Chances are good that any call for avocado is to use it as a dressing or sauce, and it will be combined with an acid, like vinegar or citrus juice, to aid in storing longer.

Finally, you won't see me suggesting you freeze pasta or potato recipes, because neither will do well frozen. Special storage tips will be included in each recipe and prep.

The Art of Storage

You've built your plant-based pantry staples, planned your first prep or two, and grocery shopped, and this week's food is cooking. It's showtime! Just how are you going to store your beautiful bounty? Two words: airtight containers.

Air is the enemy when storing food. After the time and care you've taken to create meals for the week, the last thing you want is food that loses its color, flavor, and texture because it wasn't stored correctly. Here are my tips for storage success:

CONTAINERS

I love having a variety of containers on hand, as some foods work in certain containers better than others.

Single- and multicompartment: Plant-based bowl meals (also known as "Buddha" or "hippie" bowls) and one-pot recipes are perfect for single-compartment glass or plastic containers. But some people have a real thing about their foods touching, and multicompartment containers usually have three spaces to store your beans, veggies, and grains separately. MealPrep sells reusable containers in packs of 15.

Stackable/nestable: If space is an issue, consider stackable containers. Stacking in the refrigerator makes it easy to see your preps and saves room. When not in use, they also take up less space in the cupboard. Prep Naturals makes stackable containers.

Plastic: A little old school, plastic bags can be pretty handy because you'll have more room in your freezer. Store cooked beans or grains in a bag, flatten the bags out, press the air out, and seal. The number of bulk-cooked foods you can freeze when the food is flat will surprise you. If you're trying to reduce plastic in your life—as so many of us are—consider investing in ecofriendly reusable food storage bags.

Glass: I adore glass jars. I use them to store dried beans and grains in the pantry, flour and seeds in the refrigerator, and homemade cubes of vegan butter in the freezer. And I also use them for meal prep. A wide-mouth pint jar is perfect for a cup of grains and a mix of beans of vegetables. If I haven't used it up by the end of the week, I just place the jar in the freezer. Quart jars are excellent for salads in a jar with so much room for the leafy greens! And even 4-ounce jars are excellent for nuts, snacks, or sauces. These containers are BPA-free.

BPA-free: Bisphenol A is a chemical once commonly used in plastic containers (and still used for more industrial-type storage). If you opt for plastic containers, look for the BPA-free symbol as you'll be using the containers frequently and food will be stored in them for up to 5 days (or even several months if frozen).

Leakproof: I tote my meal preps in a bag when I head to the office, and I do not want to find tomato sauce on my laptop! That's one reason I tend to use glass jars and containers with airtight lids. Keep this in mind when you're deciding which container to use for a prep. Something soupy or saucy needs a good lid! Prep Naturals makes a backpack that holds three prep containers in an insulated section and also has a computer sleeve.

Microwave-/dishwasher-/freezer-safe: This is a must! You're meal prepping to save time, so get the container that suits this need. Glass containers are perfect for the microwave (take off the lid if using a jar!), dishwasher, and freezer. When selecting a plastic storage container, be sure to read the label to ensure it can hold up to all three.

For any type of container, remember that each recipe will indicate the recommended storage time and location.

SMART LABELING

It's worth mentioning again: Whether storing batch-cooked food in the freezer or a weekly meal prep in the refrigerator, label the container with the contents and date.

THAWING AND REHEATING

The recipes and meal preps can be stored in the refrigerator and consumed in about 5 days. In most cases, simply microwaving the prep for 2 to 3 minutes or transferring to a saucepan and heating on medium-low on the stove for 8 to 10 minutes will do the trick.

Of course sometimes life gets in the way and you don't eat all of your preps. Or you may get ambitious and double a recipe. That's when you freeze. When you're ready to heat, you're going to need to thaw and then reheat. The

VEGAN PRESSURE COOKING

You can't possibly be surprised that I'm going to bring up the Instant Pot and pressure cooking! I wrote the cookbook *Vegan Pressure Cooking*, after all. Beans and whole grains—two foods that when cooked from dry can take some time—cook up quickly and beautifully in a pressure cooker. The Instant Pot is becoming a standard appliance in many homes, and its pressure-cooking function gets used the most. I make a point throughout the book to note when an Instant Pot or pressure cooker might help you get a recipe or prep together a little more quickly. In addition to cooking food fast, you'll save money because buying dried beans and whole grains in bulk is considerably cheaper than in cans and boxes. If you decide to batch cook beans via pressure cooking, use 1½ cups cooked beans whenever a recipe calls for canned beans.

best way to thaw is to simply transfer the prep from the freezer to the refrigerator overnight before heating. If you're in a hurry, a cold-water thaw is another option. Run cold water in a bowl and place the container inside. Add more cold water as needed. While thawing in the microwave is an option, I don't recommend it. It often reheats unevenly, cooking food at the sides and leaving it frozen in the middle.

This Book's Recipes and Meal Preps

This book is laid out to achieve two goals: prep ease and vegan cooking success.

The rest of this chapter is all about prepping. I provide eight 5-day meal preps designed for one person to use. Each has a different thematic focus and balance of recipes.

Prep 1: Grain Goodness (2 breakfasts and 2 snacks): Learn to incorporate hearty and healthy whole grains into your everyday meals.

Prep 2: Beat the Heat (1 breakfast, 2 snacks, and 1 lunch): This prep is fantastic in the summer (no cooking!) or anytime you want to spend a little less time getting ready for the week.

Prep 3: Go Green (1 breakfast, 2 snacks, and 2 lunches): You'll often hear "Eat the rainbow!" when one describes how to eat a vegan diet. Green is a color that deserves great focus, and you'll get that here.

Prep 4: For the Love of Legumes (2 lunches and 2 snacks): Going vegan often means adding a food that wasn't a big part of our diets: beans. This prep demonstrates the wide variety of legumes—and ways to prepare them.

Prep 5: To the East (3 lunches/dinners and 1 snack): I believe the secret ingredient to vegan cooking is "umami"—the fifth flavor in Japanese cuisine. You'll learn all about it in this prep.

Prep 6: Fiesta Time (3 lunches/dinners and 2 snacks): Continuing our global journey, the flavors in this prep are a nod to Mexican cuisine.

Prep 7: Beautiful Bowls (4 lunches/dinners and 1 snack): When all else fails and culinary creativity is elusive, build a bowl!

Prep 8: Back to Basics: (1 breakfast, 3 lunches/dinners, and 1 snack): New vegans often miss foods they grew up with. This prep focuses on plant-based and healthier versions of some of those foods.

In each prep I will guide you from start to finish so you can complete a week's prep efficiently. Hopefully the hardest thing you'll have to do is decide which one to use! And to make that decision, simply think about the meals you need most in the next week and consider the amount of time required to prep before selecting the one that is right for you.

In part 2, you'll find recipes that are excellent for meal preps and batch cooking. As meal prepping becomes your new habit, there's a good chance you'll just start choosing the recipes you love and prepping accordingly. I will provide serving suggestions along with storage tips and nutritional information for each recipe.

You will find a special recipe index (page 140) with indications to show you which recipes are gluten-, nut-, or oil-free, or provide options to make them so.

Okay, let's prep!

ANATOMY OF A MASON JAR SALAD

You already know I love glass jars for food and meal prep storage. But did you know that mason jars are also great for salads? It's all about how you layer the ingredients, because no one wants a soggy salad! Remember that wide-mouth jars are key (you need lots of room to pack in all the good stuff), and I prefer a quart jar for salads.

1. Begin with your dressing or nut sauce.
2. Add diced cucumbers, onion, scallions, or jicama to the dressing.
3. Next, add foods that will do well soaking up the dressing: tofu, beans, mushrooms, diced zucchini, and so on.
4. For a heartier meal, add a cooked grain; farro, quinoa, and barley are excellent in salads.
5. If using nuts or seeds, add them now.
6. And now it's time to stuff the jar with your raw leafy green of choice: lettuce, spinach, kale, arugula, or any combination of the four.

To eat, I like to simply turn the jar upside down over a large bowl or a plate. Try this method with Cowboy Caviar Salad (pictured here, recipe on page 80), Red Bean and Corn Salad (page 74), or Cucumber and Onion Quinoa Salad (page 85).

GRAIN GOODNESS

Throughout the book I reiterate the basics of plant-based eating—the Fab Five: vegetables, fruit, legumes and beans, grains, and nuts and seeds. I also coach you through the recipes to help you prepare basic meal preps. Now we're bringing it all together so that when you have time to spend a couple of hours in the kitchen, the result will be a series of preps ready to roll for the week.

We're starting with a prep that many people crave as a new vegan: breakfast and snack ideas. The theme of this prep is grains—because they are such an important part of a plant-based diet. But remember as you plan your meals each day to make sure you're including foods from all of the Fab Five. And note that pancakes and pinwheels pack protein-powered legumes and veggies.

RECIPES

Pumpkin Steel-Cut Oats (page 54)

Savory Pancakes (page 64)

Veggie Hummus Pinwheels (page 133)

Baked Granola (page 134)

◀◀ Veggie Hummus Pinwheels (page 133)

SHOPPING LIST

OILS AND ACIDS
- Lemon juice
- Nonstick cooking spray
- Olive oil

HERBS AND SPICES
- Garlic salt
- Onion powder
- Salt

PRODUCE
- Carrots (2)
- Leafy greens (arugula, spinach, or baby kale) (3 ounces)
- Mushrooms (3 ounces)
- Onion (1)
- Swiss chard leaves (3)

NUTS, SEEDS, DRIED FRUIT
- Cherries, dried
- Pumpkin seeds (pepitas)
- Sesame seeds
- Walnuts

GRAINS
- Rolled oats
- Steel-cut oats
- Tortillas (whole-grain, spinach, or gluten-free)
- Whole-wheat flour

CANNED, DRIED, AND PACKAGED GOODS
- Hummus (1 [8-ounce] package)
- Plant-based milk, unsweetened (1 [8-ounce] container)
- Pumpkin purée (1 [8-ounce] can)
- Tofu, soft (1 [14-ounce] package)

OTHER
- Baking soda
- Maple syrup

EQUIPMENT
- Baking sheet
- Blender or food processor
- Chef's knife
- Cutting board
- Large saucepan
- Measuring cups and spoons
- Mixing bowls
- Skillet or griddle pan
- Spatula
- Storage containers

STEP-BY-STEP PREP

1. Prepare the Baked Granola (page 134) through step 3.

2. Once the granola is in the oven, prepare the Pumpkin Steel-Cut Oats (page 54) through step 2.

3. While the granola and oats are cooking, make the Veggie Hummus Pinwheels (page 133) in their entirety and place in 3 storage containers. Store in the refrigerator.

4. Prepare the Savory Pancakes (page 64) through step 3.

5. Finish the Pumpkin Steel-Cut Oats (steps 3 and 4). Scoop ¾ cup of oatmeal into each of 4 single-serving containers or wide-mouth pint jars. Place 3 servings in the refrigerator and the fourth in the freezer.

	Breakfast	Snack
DAY 1	Pumpkin Steel-Cut Oats	Veggie Hummus Pinwheels
DAY 2	Savory Pancakes	Veggie Hummus Pinwheels
DAY 3	Pumpkin Steel-Cut Oats	Veggie Hummus Pinwheels
DAY 4	Savory Pancakes	Baked Granola
DAY 5	Pumpkin Steel-Cut Oats	Baked Granola

6. Remove the granola from the oven and place 1 cup of granola into each of 2 containers (or transfer to 1 large airtight container) and store at room temperature. Store the remaining granola in a freezer bag in the freezer for up the three months.

7. Finish cooking the Savory Pancakes (step 4). Evenly divide the pancakes into four stacks. For the week, use 2 storage containers and place one stack in each; store in the refrigerator. For the other two stacks, layer a piece of parchment paper between each pancake, then store them in a large plastic freezer bag and place in the freezer.

BEAT THE HEAT

This meal prep is perfect during hot summer days or weeks when you want everything to come together fast—I'm talking 45-minutes-for-four-recipes fast, friends! There is no cooking involved. Can you believe it? We're using a variety of fruits and vegetables for the soup and salad, and we're using grains and nuts in the breakfast and snacks. So as you round out your well-balanced eating for the week, focus on adding your favorite plant-based proteins and lots of greens. And if you want to bulk up your chilled soup, notice the recipe tip where I walk you through a quick—no cooking required—tofu feta to serve in the soup. Note that you'll have extra servings of Spicy Fruit and Veggie Gazpacho and Minty Fruit Salad; freezing suggestions are noted in the step-by-step prep.

RECIPES

Cinnamon and Spice Overnight Oats (page 56)

Spicy Fruit and Veggie Gazpacho (page 97)

Cashew-Chocolate Truffles (page 136)

Minty Fruit Salad (page 137)

≪ Cinnamon and Spice Overnight Oats (page 56)

SHOPPING LIST

OILS AND ACIDS

- Coconut oil
- Lemon juice
- Olive oil
- Unseasoned rice vinegar

HERBS AND SPICES

- Black peppercorns
- Cinnamon, ground
- Ginger, ground
- Salt

PRODUCE

- Bell pepper, red (1)
- Blueberries (1 pint)
- Cucumber (1)
- Dill, fresh (1 bunch)
- Mint, fresh (1 bunch)
- Onion, red (1)
- Pineapple (1)
- Raspberries (1 pint)
- Serrano chile (1)
- Strawberries (1 pint)
- Tomatoes, large (2)
- Watermelon, small (1)

NUTS, SEEDS, DRIED FRUIT

- Cashews
- Dates
- Pecans
- Pumpkin seeds (pepitas)
- Shredded coconut, unsweetened

GRAINS

- Old-fashioned rolled oats

CANNED, DRIED, AND PACKAGED GOODS

- Plant-based milk, unsweetened
  (1 [32-ounce] container plus
  1 [8-ounce] container)

OTHER

- Cocoa powder
- Maple syrup

EQUIPMENT

- Baking sheet
- Blender or food processor
- Chef's knife
- Cutting board
- Measuring cups and spoons
- Mixing bowl
- Storage containers

STEP-BY-STEP PREP

1. Prepare the Cinnamon and Spice Overnight Oats (page 56) in its entirety, placing the prepared oats directly into 5 wide-mouth jars or storage containers. Place in the refrigerator.

2. Prepare the Minty Fruit Salad (page 137) in its entirety, and portion it into 2 storage containers and 2 plastic freezer bags. Store the meal prep containers in the refrigerator. Store the plastic bags in the freezer and use the frozen fruit in a future smoothie.

	Breakfast	Lunch	Snack
DAY 1	Cinnamon and Spice Overnight Oats	Spicy Fruit and Veggie Gazpacho	Minty Fruit Salad
DAY 2	Cinnamon and Spice Overnight Oats	Spicy Fruit and Veggie Gazpacho	Minty Fruit Salad
DAY 3	Cinnamon and Spice Overnight Oats	Spicy Fruit and Veggie Gazpacho	Cashew-Chocolate Truffles
DAY 4	Cinnamon and Spice Overnight Oats	Spicy Fruit and Veggie Gazpacho	Cashew-Chocolate Truffles
DAY 5	Cinnamon and Spice Overnight Oats	Spicy Fruit and Veggie Gazpacho	Cashew-Chocolate Truffles

3. Make the Spicy Fruit and Veggie Gazpacho (page 97) in its entirety. Pour 2-cup servings into each of 5 storage containers and place in the refrigerator. Pour the remaining gazpacho into a sturdy, large plastic freezer bag. Label and freeze for up to 3 months.

4. Make the Cashew-Chocolate Truffles (page 136) in its entirety, and measure out 3 or 4 truffles into each of 3 storage containers (or place all the truffles in a large container) and store in the refrigerator. Place the remaining truffles in a plastic freezer bag and store in the freezer.

Prep Three

GO GREEN

Get your engines started! We'll be using three burners on your stove this week, but nothing cooks for longer than 35 or 40 minutes! This verdant prep is all about showcasing leafy greens and how they add color and varying textures to plant-based staples. With two extra servings of Mediterranean Beans with Greens and three extra Italian Lentils, you'll basically have food for breakfast, lunch, *and* dinner this week (but I'll still provide freezing instructions in the step-by-step prep).

RECIPES

Tofu-Spinach Scramble (page 62)

Mediterranean Beans with Greens (page 75)

Italian Lentils (page 103)

Kale Chips (page 127)

« Mediterranean Beans with Greens (page 75)

SHOPPING LIST

OILS AND ACIDS
* Lemon juice
* Olive oil

HERBS AND SPICES
* Basil, dried
* Bay leaf
* Black peppercorns
* Chili powder
* Chipotle powder
* Cumin, ground
* Oregano, dried
* Rosemary, dried
* Thyme, dried
* Turmeric, ground
* Salt
* Smoked paprika

PRODUCE
* Apples, Granny Smith (3)
* Arugula (10 ounces)
* Carrots (2)
* Celery (3 stalks)
* Kale (1 bunch)
* Onion, yellow (1)
* Romaine lettuce (3 heads)
* Spinach (20 ounces)

CANNED, DRIED, AND PACKAGED GOODS
* Cannellini beans (2 [14.5-ounce] cans)
* Diced tomatoes (1 [28-ounce] can)
* French or brown lentils, dried (18 ounces)
* Green olives (1 [2.25-ounce] can)
* Minced garlic (1 [4.5-ounce] jar)
* Vegetable broth (1 [8-ounce] carton)

OTHER
* Nut butter (1 jar)
* Tofu, extra-firm (1 [14-ounce] package)

EQUIPMENT
* Baking sheet
* Chef's knife
* Cutting board
* Large pot
* Measuring cups and spoons
* Mixing bowl
* Saucepan
* Skillet
* Storage containers

STEP-BY-STEP PREP

1. Preheat the oven to 275°F.

2. Prepare the Italian Lentils (page 103) through step 2.

3. Prepare the Kale Chips (page 127) through step 3.

4. Prepare the Tofu-Spinach Scramble (page 62) through step 4.

5. Begin the Mediterranean Beans with Greens (page 75) through step 1.

6. Return to the Tofu-Spinach Scramble for step 5.

7. Return to the Mediterranean Beans with Greens for step 2.

	Breakfast	Lunch	Snack
DAY 1	Tofu-Spinach Scramble	Italian Lentils chopped salad	Kale Chips
DAY 2	Tofu-Spinach Scramble	Italian Lentils chopped salad	Kale Chips
DAY 3	Tofu-Spinach Scramble	Mediterranean Beans with Greens	Granny Smith apple with nut butter
DAY 4	Tofu-Spinach Scramble	Italian Lentils chopped salad	Granny Smith apple with nut butter
DAY 5	Tofu-Spinach Scramble	Mediterranean Beans with Greens	Granny Smith apple with nut butter

8. Remove the Kale Chips from the oven. Divide evenly between 2 wide-mouth glass jars or single-compartment containers and store at room temperature.

9. Drain the lentils and transfer to a bowl to cool at room temperature or in the refrigerator.

10. Transfer the Tofu-Spinach Scramble, evenly distributing among 5 single-compartment storage containers. Place in the refrigerator.

11. Finish the Mediterranean Beans with Greens by spooning the sautéed arugula into 4 airtight containers, then adding the beans over the arugula. Store 2 containers in the refrigerator and 2 servings in the freezer.

12. To make Italian Lentils chopped salad, shred or chop 3 heads of romaine lettuce. Spoon 1 cup of cooled (or cold) lentils into a wide-mouth quart jar. Top with ⅓ of the chopped lettuce. Repeat two more times and place the jars in the refrigerator. Transfer the remaining lentils to a large, sturdy plastic freezer bag and place in the freezer.

FOR THE LOVE OF LEGUMES

If you're like me, you weren't born a vegan. Nor was I raised eating many beans or legumes. So as I started my plant-based culinary journey, it meant learning to know, love, and prepare a variety of beans and legumes. In this week's meal prep, I want you to see the varied ways to prepare legumes. Speaking of which, did you know quinoa is an honorary legume? The lysine helps make this grain (seed, actually) a great source of protein. In this prep you'll have two extra servings of Mashed Potatoes and Kale with White Beans; consider forming those into two patties and baking or frying them as fun veggie burgers. There will also be two extra servings of the Quinoa and Kale Bowl. You can have them for dinner or freeze them.

RECIPES

Mashed Potatoes and Kale with White Beans (page 70)

Quinoa and Kale Bowl (page 81)

White Bean and Sun-dried Tomato Dip (page 115)

Roasted Chickpeas (page 131)

◀◀ Quinoa and Kale Bowl (page 81)

SHOPPING LIST

OILS AND ACIDS
- Lemon juice
- Olive oil

HERBS AND SPICES
- Black peppercorns
- Garlic powder
- Salt
- Smoked paprika

PRODUCE
- Baby carrots (1 [32-ounce] bag)
- Cucumber (1)
- Kale (12 ounces)
- Russet potatoes, large (2)
- Tomato (1)
- Zucchini (1)

GRAINS
- Quinoa

CANNED, DRIED, AND PACKAGED GOODS
- Cannellini beans (1 [14.5-ounce] can)
- Chickpeas (1 [14.5-ounce] can)
- Great northern or navy beans (1 [14.5-ounce] can)
- Minced garlic (1 [4.5-ounce] jar)
- Sun-dried tomatoes, oil-packed (1 [3-ounce] jar)
- Vegetable broth (1 [8-ounce] carton)

EQUIPMENT
- Baking sheet
- Chef's knife
- Colander
- Cutting board
- Food processor or blender
- Large pot
- Measuring cups and spoons
- Mixing bowl
- Potato masher or small handheld blender
- Saucepan
- Storage containers

STEP-BY-STEP PREP

1. Preheat the oven to 425°F.

2. Prepare the Mashed Potatoes and Kale with White Beans (page 70) through step 1.

3. Prepare the Quinoa and Kale Bowl (page 81) through step 1.

4. Prepare the Roasted Chickpeas (page 131) through step 3.

5. Return to the Mashed Potatoes and Kale with White Beans for step 2.

6. Return to the Quinoa and Kale Bowl for step 2.

7. Check on the chickpeas 15 minutes into roasting.

	Lunch	Snack
DAY 1	Mashed Potatoes and Kale with White Beans	Roasted Chickpeas
DAY 2	Quinoa and Kale Bowl	Roasted Chickpeas
DAY 3	Mashed Potatoes and Kale with White Beans	White Bean and Sundried Tomato Dip with raw veggies
DAY 4	Quinoa and Kale Bowl	White Bean and Sundried Tomato Dip with raw veggies
DAY 5	Mashed Potatoes and Kale with White Beans	White Bean and Sundried Tomato Dip with raw veggies

8. Continue with step 3 of the Mashed Potatoes and Kale with White Beans. Divide into 4 servings. Distribute 2 servings into single-compartment containers and place in the refrigerator. If you want to freeze the remaining 2 servings, form them into patties and store them in a freezer bag in the freezer. These can be thawed and baked or fried as veggie patties in the future.

9. Turn the oven off to let the chickpeas cool as described in step 4 of Roasted Chickpeas. Use the remaining chickpeas as a crouton alternative on salads or as a garnish for soup.

10. Distribute the Quinoa and Kale Bowl mixture equally into 4 single-compartment containers. Place the containers in the refrigerator, or freeze 2 containers for later.

11. Prepare the White Bean and Sun-dried Tomato Dip (page 115) entirely. Transfer ½ cup into each of 3 small airtight containers and store in the refrigerator.

12. Cut a zucchini into sticks and a cucumber into slices. Together with baby carrots, prepare 3 containers or plastic bags of raw vegetables for the dip and store in the refrigerator.

TO THE EAST

Flavor profiles, and learning how to use and adapt them, are a big part of mastering vegan cooking. I'm a huge fan of Asian-inspired (East and South) tastes. They are filled with umami—the "fifth flavor" that brings out the meatiness and savoriness in all foods, including plants. In the Easy Kitchari recipe and on the shopping list, you'll see that I call for "chopped vegetables." I do this intentionally—but with some suggestions—because it's a great way to use up vegetables in the crisper. Check your refrigerator and produce bowls before buying more vegetables! Finally, in this meal prep we have lots of food, plenty for lunch and dinner all week long.

RECIPES

Sweet Tamari Tempeh with Roasted Vegetables (page 68)

Easy Kitchari (page 82)

Red Pepper Lentils (page 104)

Tamari Almonds (page 130)

« Sweet Tamari Tempeh with Roasted Vegetables (page 68)

SHOPPING LIST

OILS AND ACIDS
- Lemon juice
- Olive oil

HERBS AND SPICES
- Black peppercorns
- Chili powder
- Coriander, ground
- Cumin, ground
- Fennel seeds
- Ginger, ground
- Salt
- Turmeric, ground

PRODUCE
- Bell peppers, red (2)
- Brussels sprouts (1 pound) or cauliflower (1 head)
- Chopped vegetables (carrot, cauliflower, summer or winter squash, broccoli, potato) (2 pounds)
- Ginger, fresh (1 inch)
- Jalapeño pepper (1)
- Lemon (1)
- Onion, red (1)
- Onion, yellow (1)
- Tomato (1)

NUTS, SEEDS, DRIED FRUIT
- Almonds
- Dates

GRAINS
- Basmati rice
- Sourdough or crusty bread loaf (1)

CANNED, DRIED, AND PACKAGED GOODS
- Diced tomatoes (1 [14.5-ounce] can)
- Minced garlic (1 [4.5-ounce] jar)
- Red lentils, dried (1 cup)
- Yellow mung beans or split peas, dried (½ cup)

OTHER
- Nutritional yeast
- Tamari or soy sauce
- Tempeh (1 [16-ounce] package)

EQUIPMENT
- Baking sheets (2)
- Blender or food processor
- Chef's knife
- Colander
- Cutting board
- Large pots (2)
- Measuring cups and spoons
- Storage containers

STEP-BY-STEP PREP

Before you begin, note that I recommend marinating the tempeh for the Sweet Tamari Tempeh with Roasted Vegetables for at least an hour, or even overnight. Consider getting some of your ingredients together the evening before prep day so you can get the most out of the marinade and a head start to cooking.

1. Preheat the oven to 400°F.

2. Begin the Easy Kitchari (page 82) through step 1.

3. Prepare the Sweet Tamari Tempeh with Roasted Vegetables (page 68) through step 3.

4. Prepare the Tamari Almonds (page 130) through step 2.

	Lunch	Dinner	Snack
DAY 1	Easy Kitchari	Sweet Tamari Tempeh with Roasted Vegetables	Tamari Almonds
DAY 2	Sweet Tamari Tempeh with Roasted Vegetables	Red Pepper Lentils with crusty bread	Tamari Almonds
DAY 3	Easy Kitchari	Red Pepper Lentils with crusty bread	Tamari Almonds
DAY 4	Red Pepper Lentils with crusty bread	Sweet Tamari Tempeh with Roasted Vegetables	Tamari Almonds
DAY 5	Sweet Tamari Tempeh with Roasted Vegetables	Red Pepper Lentils with crusty bread	Tamari Almonds

5. Return to the Easy Kitchari for steps 2 through 5.

6. Remove the almonds from the oven to cool.

7. Return to the Sweet Tamari Tempeh with Roasted Vegetables after 25 minutes for step 4.

8. Prepare the Red Pepper Lentils (page 104) through step 1.

9. Transfer the Easy Kitchari into 5 single-serving containers and place 2 servings in the refrigerator and 3 servings in the freezer.

10. Add the lemon juice to finish the Red Pepper Lentils, transfer to 4 single-serving containers, and place in the refrigerator.

11. Transfer the Sweet Tamari Tempeh with Roasted Vegetables to 4 single-serving containers and place in the refrigerator.

12. Finish step 3 for the Tamari Almonds. To store, transfer 3 servings to a large plastic bag and freeze. Divide the other half into 5 servings and store in airtight containers or plastic storage bags at room temperature.

FIESTA TIME

Moving on to yet another flavor profile perfect for plant-based cooking, we're going south of the border with my takes on Mexican dishes. In these recipes, you'll find cumin, chili powder, and paprika—all ingredients that bring a spicy, umami element. Again, to get you used to how to cook vegan on the regular, I want you to see how versatile beans are and how you can use a flavor profile that never tires. While this prep calls for only two baked potatoes, make three or more and use them in any of the lunches and dinners this week if you're looking for a bigger meal. So as you look at the number of recipes, don't fear! They are very easy. You've got this!

Note: You'll use a spiced version of Cashew Cream both for the Red Bean and Corn Salad and for your snacks. Prepper's choice: tortilla chips, raw veggies, or both? You decide!

RECIPES

Red Bean and Corn Salad (page 74)

Basic Baked Potatoes (page 99)

Peppered Pinto Beans (page 102)

Spanish Rice (page 110)

Cashew Cream (page 122)

Taco Pita Pizzas (page 128)

« Peppered Pinto Beans (page 102) and Spanish Rice (page 110)

SHOPPING LIST

OILS AND ACIDS

- Lemon juice
- Olive oil
- Unseasoned rice vinegar or apple cider vinegar

HERBS AND SPICES

- Black peppercorns
- Chili powder
- Cumin, ground
- Paprika
- Salt

PRODUCE

- Bell pepper, red (1)
- Jalapeños (2)
- Mushrooms (4 ounces)
- Onion (1)
- Romaine lettuce (3 heads)
- Russet potatoes (2)
- Tomato (1)
- Vegetables for snacking (baby carrots, celery, cucumber, radishes) (8 ounces to 1 pound)

NUTS, SEEDS, DRIED FRUIT

- Cashews, raw

GRAINS

- Sandwich-size pitas or Sandwich Thins (4)
- Short-grain brown rice
- Tortilla chips (1 [3-ounce] bag)

CANNED, DRIED, AND PACKAGED GOODS

- Kidney beans (2 [14.5-ounce] cans)
- Minced garlic (1 [4.5-ounce] jar)
- Pinto beans (2 [14.5-ounce] cans)
- Pizza sauce (1 [8-ounce] can)
- Refried beans (1 [14.5-ounce] can)
- Tomato paste (1 [6-ounce] can)
- Vegetable broth (1 [32-ounce] carton)

OTHER

- Frozen corn (1 [16-ounce] bag)

EQUIPMENT

- Baking sheet
- Blender or food processor
- Chef's knife
- Cutting board
- Large pot
- Measuring cups and spoons
- Saucepan
- Storage containers

STEP-BY-STEP PREP

Before you begin, note that the cashews should be soaked for 1 hour.

1. Preheat the oven to 400°F.

2. Begin preparing the Spanish Rice (page 110) through step 1.

3. Prepare the Basic Baked Potatoes (page 99) through step 2.

4. Begin the Peppered Pinto Beans (page 102) through step 1.

5. Prepare the Red Bean and Corn Salad (page 74) in its entirety and refrigerate the jars.

6. Remove the Spanish Rice from the stove top after 45 minutes.

7. Prepare the Taco Pita Pizzas (page 128) through step 3.

	Lunch	Dinner	Snack
DAY 1	Peppered Pinto Beans and Spanish Rice	Red Bean and Corn Salad	Taco Pita Pizza
DAY 2	Red Bean and Corn Salad	Peppered Pinto Beans and Basic Baked Potato	Taco Pita Pizza
DAY 3	Peppered Pinto Beans and Spanish Rice	Red Bean and Corn Salad	Cashew Cream and chips or vegetables
DAY 4	Peppered Pinto Beans and Spanish Rice	Red Bean and Corn Salad	Cashew Cream and chips or vegetables
DAY 5	Basic Baked Potato (with your favorite toppings, like vegan butter, vegan sour cream, and chives)	Peppered Pinto Beans and Spanish Rice	Cashew Cream and chips or vegetables

8. Remove the pinto beans from the stove. Into each of 2 storage containers, spoon ⅓ cup of beans. Refrigerate one and freeze the other.

9. Remove the potatoes from the oven when cooked through.

10. Prepare the Cashew Cream (page 122) through step 2. Transfer to a glass jar and store in the refrigerator.

11. If using raw vegetables for your snack, wash, chop or slice, and place them in 3 storage containers or plastic snack bags.

12. Fluff the Spanish Rice and spoon 1 cup into each of 4 storage containers along with ⅓ cup of pinto beans. Place the containers in the refrigerator.

13. Remove the pita pizzas from the oven and cool completely before storing in individual storage containers for each pizza, or stack, with parchment paper between each pizza, in a large plastic bag. Refrigerate 2 pizzas and freeze the other 2 servings for later.

14. Store the potatoes in a large plastic bag or airtight storage container in the refrigerator.

BEAUTIFUL BOWLS

Have you heard of "Buddha" or "hippie" bowls? It's a play on the stereotype that hippies eat beans, greens, and grains. Well, first of all, sounds good to me. But, more importantly, everyone is eating one-stop bowl-style meals these days (think Chipotle) because it's an easy way to repurpose leftovers and meet all your nutrient goals for the day. The bowls in this prep feature legumes, grains, veggies (lots of 'em), and fruit, all to demonstrate that it's really quite simple to serve yourself—and your family—balanced meals easily.

RECIPES

Green Pea Risotto (page 69)

Warm Vegetable "Salad" (page 72)

Cucumber and Onion Quinoa Salad (page 85)

Chickpea and Artichoke Curry (page 87)

Parm-y Kale Pesto (page 114)

Minty Fruit Salad (page 137)

« Chickpea and Artichoke Curry (page 87)

SHOPPING LIST

OILS AND ACIDS

- Lemon juice
- Olive oil
- White wine vinegar

HERBS AND SPICES

- Black peppercorns
- Coriander, ground
- Cumin, ground
- Curry powder
- Dill, dried
- Salt

PRODUCE

- Blueberries, fresh (½ pint)
- Carrots (1½ pounds)
- Celery (1 stalk)
- Cucumber, large (1)
- Dill, fresh (1 bunch)
- Kale (5 ounces)
- Lettuce (romaine, iceberg, or green or red leaf) (1 pound)
- Lime (1)
- Mint, fresh (1 bunch)
- Onion, any type, small (1)
- Onion, sweet, large (1)
- Pineapple (1)
- Raspberries (1 pint)
- Red potatoes (4)
- Strawberries (1 pint)

NUTS, SEEDS, DRIED FRUIT

- Walnuts

GRAINS

- Arborio rice
- Quinoa

CANNED, DRIED, AND PACKAGED GOODS

- Artichokes (1 [14.5-ounce] can)
- Chickpeas (1 [14.5-ounce] can)
- Coconut milk (1 [5.4-ounce] can)
- Hummus (1 [8-ounce] package)
- Minced garlic (1 [4.5-ounce] jar)
- Vegetable broth or not-chicken broth (1 [16-ounce] can)

OTHER

- Frozen peas (1 [16-ounce] bag)
- Maple syrup
- Nutritional yeast
- Vegan butter (1 [8-ounce] container)
- Vegan sugar

EQUIPMENT

- Chef's knife
- Cutting board
- Food processor
- Large pot
- Large skillets (2)
- Measuring cups and spoons
- Medium pot or saucepan
- Storage containers

STEP-BY-STEP PREP

1. Begin the Green Pea Risotto (page 69) through step 1.

2. Prepare the Warm Vegetable "Salad" (page 72) through step 1.

3. Begin the Cucumber and Onion Quinoa Salad (page 85) through step 1.

4. Add the carrots to the boiling potatoes for the vegetable salad.

	Lunch	Dinner	Snack
DAY 1	Chickpea and Artichoke Curry	Warm Vegetable "Salad" with Parm-y Kale Pesto	Minty Fruit Salad
DAY 2	Cucumber and Onion Quinoa Salad	Green Pea Risotto	Minty Fruit Salad
DAY 3	Warm Vegetable "Salad" with Parm-y Kale Pesto	Chickpea and Artichoke Curry	Minty Fruit Salad
DAY 4	Green Pea Risotto	Warm Vegetable "Salad" with Parm-y Kale Pesto	Minty Fruit Salad
DAY 5	Warm Vegetable "Salad" with Parmy-Kale Pesto	Cucumber and Onion Quinoa Salad	Hummus with carrot and celery sticks

5. Prepare the Chickpea and Artichoke Curry (page 87) through step 2.

6. Return to the Green Pea Risotto for step 2. Into each of 2 single-serving containers, scoop 1½ cups. Store the remainder in the refrigerator or freezer in airtight containers or bags.

7. Return to the Cucumber and Onion Quinoa Salad for steps 2 through 4. Set aside to cool.

8. Transfer the Chickpea and Artichoke Curry to 4 storage containers. Let cool and refrigerate 2 servings; freeze 2 servings.

9. Prepare the Parm-y Kale Pesto (page 114) completely.

10. Assemble the Warm Vegetable "Salad" in 4 containers by evenly distributing the vegetables. Then scoop ¼ cup of Parm-y Kale Pesto over the vegetables in each container. Place the containers in the refrigerator.

11. Assemble the Cucumber and Onion Quinoa Salad in 4 wide-mouth quart jars as in step 5 of the recipe. Cover and refrigerate.

12. Assemble the Minty Fruit Salad (page 137) and refrigerate.

BACK TO BASICS

The bottom line when it comes to vegan cooking is that you want to explore new ingredients and recipes *and* you want to create healthy, plant-based versions of foods you know and love. This week's prep is all about this. We're starting with a barley bowl for breakfast. We all know about oats, but there are so many breakfast grains to choose from. Polenta is inherently nonvegan, but with a few creative twists, you'll get a creamy meal without the cream, and the same goes for mac 'n' cheese (who needs cheese?). Caesar-Style Dressing is a great stand-in for ranch dip when snacking on veggies, and you can easily add a side salad to either the polenta or mac 'n' cheese and use it as a dressing.

RECIPES

« Cowboy Caviar Salad (page 80)

SHOPPING LIST

OILS AND ACIDS

- Lemon juice
- Olive oil
- Red wine vinegar
- Unseasoned rice vinegar, apple cider vinegar, or white wine vinegar

HERBS AND SPICES

- Black peppercorns
- Cumin, ground
- Oregano, dried
- Salt
- Turmeric, ground

PRODUCE

- Avocado (2)
- Bell pepper, green (1)
- Bell pepper, red (1)
- Leafy greens (kale, spinach, arugula, or romaine) (20 ounces)
- Mushrooms, any type (6 ounces)
- Red onion (1)
- Tomato, large (1)

NUTS, SEEDS, DRIED FRUIT

- Dried cranberries
- Slivered almonds

GRAINS

- Cornmeal
- Pearl barley
- Vegan elbow macaroni

CANNED, DRIED, AND PACKAGED GOODS

- Black beans (1 [14.5-ounce] can)
- Black-eyed peas (1 [14.5-ounce] can)
- Minced garlic (1 [4.5-ounce] jar)
- Vanilla plant-based milk, sweetened (1 [32-ounce] carton)
- Vegetable broth (1 [32-ounce] carton)
- Yellow corn (1 [14.5-ounce] can)

OTHER

- Dijon mustard
- Nutritional yeast
- Vegan butter (1 [8-ounce] container)
- Vegan mayonnaise
- Vegan Worcestershire sauce

EQUIPMENT

- Blender or food processor
- Chef's knife
- Cutting board
- Large pot
- Large saucepans (2)
- Measuring cups and spoons
- Mixing bowl
- Storage containers

STEP-BY-STEP PREP

1. Prepare the Barley Breakfast Bowl (page 57) through step 1.

2. Prepare the Cheesy Mushroom Polenta (page 76) through step 1.

3. Prepare the Healthy Mac 'n' Cheese (page 86) through step 1.

4. Prepare the Cowboy Caviar Salad (page 80) through step 2.

5. Return to the Cheesy Mushroom Polenta to complete steps 2 and 3. Evenly divide the polenta among 6 single-serving storage containers. Place 3 servings in the refrigerator

	Breakfast	Lunch	Dinner	Snack
DAY 1	Barley Breakfast Bowl	Cheesy Mushroom Polenta	Cowboy Caviar Salad	Raw vegetables with Caesar-Style Dressing
DAY 2	Barley Breakfast Bowl	Healthy Mac 'n' Cheese	Cheesy Mushroom Polenta	Raw vegetables with Caesar-Style Dressing
DAY 3	Barley Breakfast Bowl	Cowboy Caviar Salad	Healthy Mac 'n' Cheese	Raw vegetables with Caesar-Style Dressing
DAY 4	Barley Breakfast Bowl	Cowboy Caviar Salad	Cheesy Mushroom Polenta	Raw vegetables with Caesar-Style Dressing
DAY 5	Barley Breakfast Bowl	Healthy Mac 'n' Cheese	Cowboy Caviar Salad	Raw vegetables with Caesar-Style Dressing

to use throughout the week and freeze 3 servings.

6. Return to the Healthy Mac 'n' Cheese for step 2. Transfer, evenly divided, into 4 storage containers. Refrigerate 3 servings and freeze 1 serving.

7. Return to the barley to assemble: Divide among 6 jars or single-serving storage containers. Add ¼ cup of dried cranberries to each. Pour ½ cup of plant-based milk into each. Add 1 teaspoon of slivered almonds to each. Refrigerate 5 jars and freeze 1 jar for later.

8. Assemble the Cowboy Caviar Salad: Spoon about 2 tablespoons of the dressing into each of 4 jars. Add about 1¼ cups of "caviar" into each jar, followed by 2 cups of leafy greens. Store in the refrigerator.

9. Prepare the Caesar-Style Dressing (page 117) and transfer to a mason jar or airtight container. Store in the refrigerator.

10. Wash and slice snacking vegetables, and store in 5 plastic bags or containers in the refrigerator.

Part Two

RECIPES

BREAKFASTS

◄◄ Cinnamon and Spice Overnight Oats (page 56)

PUMPKIN STEEL-CUT OATS

MAKES 4 SERVINGS

Prep: 2 minutes / Cook: 35 minutes

It's easy to get into an oatmeal rut simply because it's a great autopilot breakfast. Adding pumpkin purée in this recipe makes for a creamier texture and brighter color. And speaking of texture, chewy pumpkin seeds (pepitas) switch things up, too. This is great with canned sweet potatoes, as well.

3 cups water

1 cup steel-cut oats

½ cup canned
   pumpkin purée

¼ cup pumpkin seeds
   (pepitas)

2 tablespoons maple syrup

Pinch salt

1. In a large saucepan, bring the water to a boil.

2. Add the oats, stir, and reduce the heat to low. Simmer until the oats are soft, 20 to 30 minutes, continuing to stir occasionally.

3. Stir in the pumpkin purée and continue cooking on low for 3 to 5 minutes longer. Stir in the pumpkin seeds and maple syrup, and season with the salt.

4. Divide the oatmeal into 4 single-serving containers. Let cool before sealing the lids.

Storage: Place the airtight containers in the refrigerator for 5 days or freeze for up to 3 months. To thaw, refrigerate overnight. Reheat in the microwave for 2½ minutes or in a skillet over medium-high heat for 6 to 8 minutes.

TIP: To cook in a pressure cooker or multicooker, such as an Instant Pot, combine all the ingredients in the pot, cover, and cook on high pressure for 5 minutes. Allow for a natural release.

Per Serving: Calories: 121; Fat: 5g; Protein: 4g; Carbohydrates: 17g; Fiber: 2g; Sugar: 7g; Sodium: 63mg

SAVORY OATMEAL PORRIDGE

MAKES 4 SERVINGS

Prep: 2 minutes / Cook: 25 minutes

How's this for getting out of that oatmeal rut? We're going savory! Porridge is a traditional hot breakfast cereal bowl. Combining three common pantry grains—rolled oats, steel-cut oats, and farro—makes this affordable and adds depth and complexity to each bite. Avoid the temptation to buy instant oats; they won't work in this recipe. I often switch up the type of vegetable broth (no-chicken or no-beef, for instance) and the plant milk, opting for what I have on hand. If you have a pressure cooker or multicooker, such as an Instant Pot, you can prepare this oatmeal in about the same amount of total time as on the stove, but without any tending. Follow the instructions, cook time, and release method as noted in the tip for Pumpkin Steel-Cut Oats (page 54).

2½ cups vegetable broth

2½ cups unsweetened almond milk or other plant-based milk

½ cup steel-cut oats

1 tablespoon farro

½ cup slivered almonds

¼ cup nutritional yeast

2 cups old-fashioned rolled oats

½ teaspoon salt (optional)

1.   In a large saucepan or pot, bring the broth and almond milk to a boil. Add the oats, farro, almond slivers, and nutritional yeast. Cook over medium-high heat for 20 minutes, stirring occasionally.

2.   Add the rolled oats and cook for another 5 minutes, until creamy. Stir in the salt (if using).

3.   Divide into 4 single-serving containers. Let cool before sealing the lids.

Storage: Place the airtight containers in the refrigerator for 5 days or freeze for up to 3 months. To thaw, refrigerate overnight. Reheat in the microwave for 2½ minutes or in a skillet over medium-high heat for 6 to 8 minutes.

TIP: To add a little umami flavor to this recipe, swap out the ½ teaspoon salt for 1 teaspoon soy sauce or gluten-free tamari.

Per Serving: Calories: 208; Fat: 8g; Protein: 14g; Carbohydrates: 22g; Fiber: 7g; Sugar: 1g; Sodium: 596mg

CINNAMON AND SPICE OVERNIGHT OATS

MAKES 5 SERVINGS

Prep: 10 minutes, plus overnight to soak

Oats really are perfect for meal prepping, but this is the recipe I never thought I'd write. Overnight oats are such the rage, and they just didn't do it for me, until I discovered that you don't actually have to use the chia seeds that are called for in most recipes. Granted, you won't get the same thickness, but for me, it's a texture thing. I'll order the tapioca pudding if I want it, but not for breakfast, thank you very much.

2½ cups old-fashioned rolled oats

5 tablespoons pumpkin seeds (pepitas)

5 tablespoons chopped pecans

5 cups unsweetened plant-based milk

2½ teaspoons maple syrup or agave syrup

½ to 1 teaspoon salt

½ to 1 teaspoon ground cinnamon

½ to 1 teaspoon ground ginger

Fresh fruit (optional)

1.   Line up 5 wide-mouth pint jars. In each jar, combine ½ cup of oats, 1 tablespoon of pumpkin seeds, 1 tablespoon of pecans, 1 cup of plant-based milk, ½ teaspoon of maple syrup, 1 pinch of salt, 1 pinch of cinnamon, and 1 pinch of ginger.

2.   Stir the ingredients in each jar. Close the jars tightly with lids. To serve, top with fresh fruit (if using).

Storage: Place the airtight jars in the refrigerator at least overnight before eating and for up to 5 days.

TIP: Any seed or nut will do. Just be sure that you use a total of ½ cup. I also love the combination of walnut and flaxseed.

Per Serving: Calories: 177; Fat: 9g; Protein: 6g; Carbohydrates: 19g; Fiber: 4g; Sugar: 3g; Sodium: 386mg

Prep Eight

BARLEY BREAKFAST BOWL

MAKES 6 SERVINGS

Prep: 5 minutes / Cook: 30 minutes

I don't know why oats tend to have all the morning glory when it comes to breakfast grains when others are just as good and offer variety to our plant-based diet. If you have another cup of barley, you can make the Pesto Pearled Barley (page 109), too!

1½ cups pearl barley

3¼ cups water

Large pinch salt

1½ cups dried cranberries or cherries

3 cups sweetened vanilla plant-based milk

2 tablespoons slivered almonds (optional)

1. In a large saucepan over high heat, combine the barley, water, and salt. Bring to a boil. Cover the pot, reduce the heat to low, and simmer for 25 to 30 minutes, stirring occasionally, until the water is absorbed.

2. Divide the barley into 6 jars or single-serving storage containers. Add ¼ cup of dried cranberries to each. Pour ½ cup of plant-based milk into each. Add 1 teaspoon of slivered almonds (if using) to each. Close the jars tightly with lids.

Storage: Place the airtight containers in the refrigerator for up to 5 days or the freezer for up to 2 months. To thaw, refrigerate overnight. Reheat in the microwave for 1½ to 3 minutes.

INGREDIENT TIP: If you prefer plain, unsweetened milk, simply combine 3 cups of it with 1 teaspoon maple syrup and ½ teaspoon vanilla extract.

PRESSURE COOKER TIP: To make the barley in an Instant Pot or pressure cooker, cook for 18 minutes on high pressure and use a quick release.

Per Serving: Calories: 249; Fat: 2g; Protein: 6g; Carbohydrates: 54g; Fiber: 9g; Sugar: 14g; Sodium: 107mg

SWEET POTATO AND BLACK BEAN HASH

Prep: 10 minutes / Cook: 25 minutes

Sweet potatoes and black beans are a match made in heaven. Nutrient dense and filling, paired they make a lovely dish. We eat with our eyes first!

1 teaspoon extra-virgin olive oil or 3 teaspoons vegetable broth

1 large sweet yellow onion, diced

2 teaspoons minced garlic (about 2 cloves)

1 large sweet potato, unpeeled, diced into ¾-inch pieces

2 teaspoons ground cumin

1 teaspoon dried oregano

1 (14.5-ounce) can black beans, rinsed and drained

¼ to ½ teaspoon salt (optional)

¼ teaspoon freshly ground black pepper

1. In large skillet over medium-high heat, heat the olive oil. Add the onion and garlic and cook for 5 minutes, stirring frequently.

2. Add the sweet potatoes, cumin, and oregano. Stir and cook for another 5 minutes. Cover the skillet, reduce the heat to low, and cook for 15 minutes.

3. After 15 minutes, increase the heat to medium-high and stir in the black beans, salt (if using), and pepper. Cook for another 5 minutes.

4. Divide evenly among 6 single-serving containers. Let cool before sealing the lids.

Storage: Place the airtight containers in the refrigerator for up to 5 days. Reheat in the microwave for 1½ to 3 minutes. Do not freeze this prep, as frigid temperatures are not ideal for cooked potatoes.

> **TIP:** For the Instant Pot or pressure cooker, use the sauté function for the first step. Then add all the remaining ingredients to the pot, cover, and cook on high pressure for 4 minutes. Use a natural release.

Per Serving: Calories: 124; Fat: 1g; Protein: 6g; Carbohydrates: 23g; Fiber: 7g; Sugar: 3g; Sodium: 14mg

GREAT GREEN SMOOTHIE

MAKES 4 SERVINGS

Prep: 5 minutes

A green smoothie is stereotypically vegan, and for good reason. Fruits, vegetables, and protein-packed nondairy milk give us everything we need in one glass! This basic formula can be changed up all kinds of ways. Always use frozen bananas (for the milkshake texture and taste), but try blueberries and kale or pineapple and romaine lettuce in place of the strawberries and spinach.

4 bananas, peeled

4 cups hulled strawberries

4 cups spinach

4 cups plant-based milk

1.   Open 4 quart-size, freezer-safe bags. In each, layer in the following order: 1 banana (halved or sliced), 1 cup of strawberries, and 1 cup of spinach. Seal and place in the freezer.

2.   To serve, take a frozen bag of Great Green Smoothie ingredients and transfer to a blender. Add 1 cup of plant-based milk, and blend until smooth.

Storage: Place freezer bags in the freezer for up to 2 months.

TIP: Freezing bananas is a great way to save them when they are browning and about to turn. I keep a gallon freezer bag in my freezer filled with halved frozen bananas. Not only can I make a smoothie on the fly, I have the base for "nice cream" (banana-based ice cream) ready to roll.

Per Serving: Calories: 173: Fat: 2g; Protein: 4g; Carbohydrates: 40g; Fiber: 7g; Sugar: 22g; Sodium: 116mg

SMOOTHIE BREAKFAST BOWL

Prep: 10 minutes

Following the basic freezer bag prep for a smoothie, we're going to add a next-level jar prep so you can pour that smoothie into a bowl and add grains and nuts (or seeds) to create a heartier—but still fast—breakfast. In this recipe I call for dragon fruit, a more affordable alternative to acai, which you will find in the frozen section at many grocery stores. Feel free to use 1 cup of your favorite fresh or frozen fruit as a substitute.

4 bananas, peeled

1 cup dragon fruit or fruit of choice

1 cup Baked Granola (page 134)

2 cups fresh berries

½ cup slivered almonds

4 cups plant-based milk

1. Open 4 quart-size, freezer-safe bags, and layer in the following order: 1 banana (halved or sliced) and ¼ cup dragon fruit.

2. Into 4 small jelly jars, layer in the following order: ¼ cup granola, ½ cup berries, and 2 tablespoons slivered almonds.

3. To serve, take a frozen bag of bananas and dragon fruit and transfer to a blender. Add 1 cup of plant-based milk, and blend until smooth. Pour into a bowl. Add the contents of 1 jar of granola, berries, and almonds over the top of the smoothie, and serve with a spoon.

Storage: Place the freezer bags in the freezer for up to 2 months. Store the jars of berries, granola, and nuts in the refrigerator for up to 1 week.

TIP: The granola, berries, and almond prep is a perfect topping for dessert! Try it over vegan ice cream or "nice cream" (puréed frozen banana).

Per Serving: Calories: 384; Fat: 9g; Protein: 6g; Carbohydrates: 57g; Fiber: 8g; Sugar: 29g; Sodium: 169mg

TORTILLA BREAKFAST CASSEROLE

MAKES 6 SERVINGS

Prep: 20 minutes / Cook: 20 minutes

I love "one-pot" meals, and casseroles certainly qualify. This is a fun way to use a traditional tofu scramble for a completely different outcome. Use the Tofu-Spinach Scramble (page 62) or another favorite scramble recipe. We almost always have this casserole in the freezer because it's a great breakfast for houseguests, and it's even good for lunch or dinner.

Nonstick cooking spray

1 recipe Tofu-Spinach Scramble (page 62)

1 (14-ounce) can black beans, rinsed and drained

¼ cup nutritional yeast

2 teaspoons hot sauce

10 small corn tortillas

½ cup shredded vegan Cheddar or pepper Jack cheese, divided

1. Preheat the oven to 350°F. Coat a 9-by-9-inch baking pan with cooking spray.

2. In a large bowl, combine the tofu scramble with the black beans, nutritional yeast, and hot sauce. Set aside.

3. In the bottom of the baking pan, place 5 corn tortillas. Spread half of the tofu and bean mixture over the tortillas. Spread ¼ cup of cheese over the top. Layer the remaining 5 tortillas over the top of the cheese. Spread the reminder of the tofu and bean mixture over the tortillas. Spread the remaining ¼ cup of cheese over the top.

4. Bake for 20 minutes.

5. Divide evenly among 6 single-serving containers. Let cool before sealing the lids.

Storage: Place the airtight containers in the refrigerator for up to 5 days or freeze for up to 3 months. To thaw, refrigerate overnight. Reheat in the microwave for 1½ to 2½ minutes.

TIP: If you want to keep the casserole intact in the freezer, consider baking it in a disposable pan. Once cool, simply cover with foil and freeze.

Per Serving: Calories: 323: Fat: 11g: Protein: 27g: Carbohydrates: 60g: Fiber: 10g: Sugar: 2g: Sodium: 146mg

TOFU-SPINACH SCRAMBLE

MAKES 5 SERVINGS

Prep: 20 minutes / Cook: 15 minutes

Tofu scramble is a staple for most vegans (and many plant-based restaurants) because it's nutrient dense and a hearty protein source. It's ideal for meal prep because it stores easily and, frankly, gets better after a few days in the refrigerator.

1 (14-ounce) package water-packed extra-firm tofu

1 teaspoon extra-virgin olive oil or ¼ cup vegetable broth

1 small yellow onion, diced

3 teaspoons minced garlic (about 3 cloves)

3 large celery stalks, chopped

2 large carrots, peeled (optional) and chopped

1 teaspoon chili powder

½ teaspoon ground cumin

½ teaspoon ground turmeric

½ teaspoon salt (optional)

¼ teaspoon freshly ground black pepper

5 cups loosely packed spinach

1. Press and drain the tofu by placing it, wrapped in a paper towel, on a plate in the sink. Place a cutting board over the tofu, then set a heavy pot, can, or cookbook on the cutting board. Remove after 10 minutes. (Alternatively, use a tofu press.)

2. In a medium bowl, crumble the tofu with your hands or a potato masher. Set aside.

3. In a large skillet over medium-high heat, heat the olive oil. Add the onion, garlic, celery, and carrots, and sauté for 5 minutes, until the onion is softened.

4. Add the crumbled tofu, chili powder, cumin, turmeric, salt (if using), and pepper, and continue cooking for 7 to 8 more minutes, stirring frequently, until the tofu begins to brown.

5. Add the spinach and mix well. Cover and reduce the heat to medium. Steam the spinach for 3 minutes.

6. Divide evenly among 5 single-serving containers. Let cool before sealing the lids.

Storage: Place the airtight containers in the refrigerator for 5 days or freeze for up to 1 month. To thaw, refrigerate overnight. Reheat in the microwave for 2½ minutes or in a skillet over medium-high heat for 6 to 8 minutes.

INGREDIENT TIP: When you want to switch up your greens, arugula, kale, and Swiss chard are great substitutes for the spinach.

TIME-SAVING TIP: Buy a ready-to-use package of prechopped carrots, celery, and onions, known (and often labeled) as *mirepoix*.

Per Serving: Calories: 170; Fat: 9g; Protein: 14g; Carbohydrates: 9g; Fiber: 3g; Sugar: 3g; Sodium: 94mg

SAVORY PANCAKES

MAKES 4 SERVINGS

Prep: 10 minutes / Cook: 15 minutes

This recipe may seem a little unconventional because we're going with savory. Why? A couple of reasons. First, I want you to get a wide variety of breakfast foods into your new plant-based routine. Second, while great in the morning, this is another meal that can easily stand in for lunch or dinner. Serve with Cashew Cream (page 122), White Bean Gravy (page 120), or your favorite prepared vegan gravy.

1 cup whole-wheat flour

1 teaspoon garlic salt

1 teaspoon onion powder

½ teaspoon baking soda

¼ teaspoon salt

1 cup lightly pressed, crumbled soft or firm tofu

⅓ cup unsweetened plant-based milk

¼ cup lemon juice (about 2 small lemons)

2 tablespoons extra-virgin olive oil

½ cup finely chopped mushrooms

½ cup finely chopped onion

2 cups tightly packed greens (arugula, spinach, or baby kale work great)

Nonstick cooking spray

1. In a large bowl, combine the flour, garlic salt, onion powder, baking soda, and salt. Mix well.

2. In a blender, combine the tofu, plant-based milk, lemon juice, and olive oil. Purée on high speed for 30 seconds.

3. Pour the contents of the blender into the bowl of dry ingredients and whisk until combined well. Fold in the mushrooms, onion, and greens.

4. Spray a large skillet or griddle pan with nonstick cooking spray and set over medium-high heat. Reduce the heat to medium and add ½ cup of batter per pancake. Cook on both sides for about 3 minutes, or until set. After flipping, press down on the cooked side of the pancake with a spatula to flatten out the pancake. Repeat until the batter is gone.

5. Divide the cooked pancakes among 4 single-serving containers. Let cool before sealing the lids.

Storage: Place the airtight storage containers in the refrigerator for up to 4 days. To reheat, microwave for 1½ to 2 minutes. To freeze, place the pancakes on a parchment paper–lined baking sheet in a single layer. If there's more than one layer, place another piece of parchment paper over the pancakes and place the second layer on top. Place the baking sheet in the freezer for 2 to 4 hours. Transfer the frozen pancakes to a freezer-safe bag (cut the parchment paper and place a small piece between each pancake). To thaw, refrigerate overnight. Preheat an oven or toaster oven to 350°F. Place the pancakes on a parchment paper–lined baking sheet and bake for 10 to 15 minutes, or stack the pancakes on a plate and microwave for 2 to 3 minutes.

> **TIP:** If you'd like to whip up fresh-cooked pancakes each morning during this prep week, transfer the pancake batter to a glass jar and just pour out what you need each morning; use the batter up within 5 days.

Per Serving: Calories: 246; Fat: 11g; Protein: 10g; Carbohydrates: 30g; Fiber: 3g; Sugar: 2g; Sodium: 367mg

LUNCHES AND DINNERS

◀◀ Quinoa and Kale Bowl (page 81)

SWEET TAMARI TEMPEH WITH ROASTED VEGETABLES

MAKES 4 SERVINGS

Prep: 10 minutes, plus at least 1 hour to marinate / Cook: 45 minutes

You've heard of one-pot meals. How about a one-sheet meal? Tempeh—the protein star of this recipe—marinated overnight is incredibly flavorful, and the roasted veggies add nutrients and a ton of flavor. If you prefer to get this done on a single prep day, skip the overnight marinating step, but do set it up first to marinate for at least an hour.

2 teaspoons extra-virgin olive oil or ¼ cup vegetable broth

2 tablespoons tamari or soy sauce

2 dates, pitted and minced

3 teaspoons minced garlic (about 3 cloves)

1 teaspoon ground ginger

1 pound tempeh, cut into bite-size pieces (about ½-inch cubes)

1 large yellow or sweet onion, cut into half-moon slices

1 large red pepper, seeded and sliced

1 pound Brussels sprouts, trimmed and halved, or 1 head cauliflower, cut into florets

1. In a medium bowl, combine the olive oil, tamari, dates, garlic, and ginger. Add the cubed tempeh, and gently toss until coated. Cover and refrigerate for 1 hour or as long as overnight.

2. Preheat the oven to 400°F.

3. Transfer the tempeh to a roasting pan. Add the onion, red pepper, and Brussels sprouts. Stir well to coat the vegetables in the marinade. Cover with foil and cook for 25 minutes.

4. Uncover and roast for another 15 to 20 minutes, until browned and tender.

5. Divide the tempeh and roasted vegetables evenly among 4 wide-mouth glass jars or single-serving containers. Let cool before sealing the lids.

Storage: Place the airtight containers in the refrigerator for up to 1 week or freeze for up to 2 months. To thaw, refrigerate overnight. Reheat in the microwave for 2 to 3 minutes.

TIP: Prep this with Baked Wild Rice (page 111).

Per Serving: Calories: 334; Fat: 15g; Protein: 27g; Carbohydrates: 31g; Fiber: 6g; Sugar: 8g; Sodium: 544mg

GREEN PEA RISOTTO

MAKES 4 SERVINGS

Prep: 5 minutes / Cook: 35 minutes

Vegan risotto is a wonder! You can achieve a creamy texture without actual heavy cream just by adding nutritional yeast and lemon juice. The green peas add a pop of color (we eat with our eyes first!) and 9 grams of protein.

1 teaspoon vegan butter

4 teaspoons minced garlic (about 4 cloves)

1 cup Arborio rice

2 cups vegetable broth (try a no-chicken broth for a richer flavor)

¼ teaspoon salt

2 tablespoons nutritional yeast

3 tablespoons lemon juice (about 1½ small lemons)

2 cups fresh, canned, or frozen (thawed) green peas

¼ to ½ teaspoon freshly ground black pepper, to taste

1. In a large skillet over medium-high heat, heat the vegan butter. Add the garlic and sauté for about 3 minutes. Add the rice, broth, and salt, and stir to combine well. Bring to boil. Reduce the heat to low and simmer for about 30 minutes, until the broth is absorbed and the rice is tender.

2. Stir in the nutritional yeast and lemon juice. Gently fold in the peas. Taste before seasoning with the pepper.

3. Divide the risotto evenly among 4 single-serving containers. Let cool before sealing the lids.

Storage: Place the airtight containers in the refrigerator for up to 5 days or freeze for up to 2 months. To thaw, refrigerate overnight. Reheat in the microwave for 1½ to 3 minutes.

TIP: Add raw arugula to 4 single-compartment storage containers and scoop the risotto over the arugula. The peppery leafy green pairs perfectly with risotto.

Per Serving: Calories: 144; Fat: 2g; Protein: 10g; Carbohydrates: 24g; Fiber: 7g; Sugar: 5g; Sodium: 273mg

MASHED POTATOES AND KALE WITH WHITE BEANS

MAKES 4 SERVINGS

Prep: 10 minutes / Cook: 30 minutes

This basic recipe is fantastic doubled, and you will notice that I'm holding back on the spices and seasonings. You can turn this into any flavor profile. My two personal favorites: dill and garlic, and chili powder and cumin. You can serve these potatoes as is with vegan gravy, *or* you can form them into patties or nuggets and bake at 425°F for 20 minutes until browned.

2 large Russet potatoes

Pinch salt (optional), plus ½ teaspoon

½ cup vegetable broth

6 ounces kale, torn into bite-size pieces

1 (14.5-ounce) can great northern beans or other white beans, rinsed and drained

¼ to ½ teaspoon freshly ground black pepper, to taste

1. Wash (but don't peel!) the potatoes, quarter them, then halve each quarter. Place in a large pot and cover with water. Add a pinch of salt (if using), and bring to a boil. Cover, reduce the heat to medium, and cook for about 20 minutes, until the potatoes are tender.

2. Drain the potatoes and return to the pot. Pour the vegetable broth over the potatoes. Add the kale and then the beans. Cover and cook on low heat for about 5 minutes, until the kale turns bright green and is lightly wilted.

3. Use a potato masher to mash everything together, and season with the ½ teaspoon salt and the pepper.

4. Divide the potatoes, kale, and beans evenly among 4 single-serving containers. Let cool before sealing the lids.

Storage: Place the airtight containers in the refrigerator for up to 5 days. Alternatively, you can form the mixture into 8 small patties or 16 round nuggets and store in a container using parchment paper between each patty or layer of nuggets.

PRESSURE COOKER TIP: Omit the water for boiling and put the potatoes, vegetable broth, kale, beans, salt, and pepper in the pot. Cover and cook on low pressure for 8 minutes. Use a quick release. Once the pressure is released, remove the lid, turn on the sauté function, and hand mash everything while the remaining liquid cooks down.

AIR FRYER TIP: "Fry" the patties or nuggets at 400°F for 8 to 10 minutes.

Per Serving: Calories: 255; Fat: 1g; Protein: 12g; Carbohydrates: 53g; Fiber: 11g; Sugar: 2g; Sodium: 98mg

WARM VEGETABLE "SALAD"

MAKES 4 SERVINGS

Prep: 10 minutes / Cook: 15 minutes

We don't usually think warm and salad go together. But really, for those of you new to vegan and plant-based cooking and eating, I want you to get creative with how you approach vegetables. Warm or cold, with sauce or dressing, there are all kinds of ways to serve them. And I think you're really going to enjoy this hot variety.

Salt for salting water, plus ½ teaspoon (optional)

4 red potatoes, quartered

1 pound carrots, sliced into ¼-inch-thick rounds

1 tablespoon extra-virgin olive oil (optional)

2 tablespoons lime juice

2 teaspoons dried dill

¼ teaspoon freshly ground black pepper

1 cup Cashew Cream (page 122) or Parm-y Kale Pesto (page 114)

1. In a large pot, bring salted water to a boil. Add the potatoes and cook for 8 minutes.

2. Add the carrots and continue to boil for another 8 minutes, until both the potatoes and carrots are crisp tender.

3. Drain and return to the pot. Add the olive oil (if using), lime juice, dill, remaining ½ teaspoon of salt (if using), and pepper, and stir to coat well.

4. Divide the vegetables evenly among 4 single-compartment storage containers or wide-mouth pint glass jars, and spoon ¼ cup of cream or pesto over the vegetables in each. Let cool before sealing the lids.

Storage: Place the airtight containers in the refrigerator for up to 1 week. To reheat, microwave for 2 minutes.

> **TIP:** Warm vegetables are delicious served over raw arugula. The tender leaves will lightly wilt just from the weight and heat of the vegetables.

Per Serving: Calories: 393; Fat: 15g; Protein: 10g; Carbohydrates: 52g; Fiber: 9g; Sugar: 8g; Sodium: 343mg

NOT-TUNA SALAD

Prep: 5 minutes

This isn't your mother's tuna salad! This version, starring chickpeas and hearts of palm, has all the flavor and texture to take you back to your childhood. If you want to make it a little "eggier," consider using black salt (which is actually pink and found at Asian or Indian markets) in place of the salt and add a pinch or two of dulse (a seaweed) flakes.

1 (15.5-ounce) can chickpeas, drained and rinsed

1 (14-ounce) can hearts of palm, drained and chopped

½ cup chopped yellow or white onion

½ cup diced celery

¼ cup vegan mayonnaise, plus more if needed

½ teaspoon salt

¼ teaspoon freshly ground black pepper

1.   In a medium bowl, use a potato masher or fork to roughly mash the chickpeas until chunky and "shredded." Add the hearts of palm, onion, celery, vegan mayonnaise, salt, and pepper. Combine and add more mayonnaise, if necessary, for a creamy texture.

2.   Into each of 4 single-serving containers, place ¾ cup of salad. Seal the lids.

Storage: Place the airtight containers in the refrigerator for up to 5 days.

TIP: Turn this into a salad jar! In a wide-mouth pint jar, add ¾ salad mix and then fill to the top with shredded lettuce or cabbage. Repeat to make 4 salad jars.

Per Serving: Calories: 214: Fat: 6g: Protein: 9g: Carbohydrates: 35g: Fiber: 8g: Sugar: 1g: Sodium: 765mg

RED BEAN AND CORN SALAD

MAKES 4 SERVINGS

Prep: 15 minutes

This combination of canned beans and frozen vegetables is proof that something tasty and wholesome can come together fast for a filling lunch or dinner on the go. Have the time? Pressure cook the beans and buy fresh corn!

¼ cup Cashew Cream (page 122) or other salad dressing

1 teaspoon chili powder

2 (14.5-ounce) cans kidney beans, rinsed and drained

2 cups frozen corn, thawed, or 2 cups canned corn, drained

1 cup cooked farro, barley, or rice (optional)

8 cups chopped romaine lettuce

1. Line up 4 wide-mouth glass quart jars.

2. In a small bowl, whisk the cream and chili powder. Pour 1 tablespoon of cream into each jar.

3. In each jar, add ¾ cup kidney beans, ½ cup corn, ¼ cup cooked farro (if using), and 2 cups romaine, punching it down to fit it into the jar. Close the lids tightly.

Storage: Place the jars in the refrigerator for up to 5 days.

TIP: If you decide to use a cooked grain, be sure to add it after the corn and before the romaine.

Per Serving: Calories: 303: Fat: 9g: Protein: 14g: Carbohydrates: 45g: Fiber: 15g; Sugar: 6g; Sodium: 654mg

MEDITERRANEAN BEANS WITH GREENS

MAKES 4 SERVINGS

Prep: 5 minutes / Cook: 10 minutes

I first shared this recipe in *Vegan for Her*, and it remains a staple in the meal planning work I do with clients because beans and greens are the perfect pairing. This balanced meal features foods commonly found in the Mediterranean diet, which is widely accepted as one of the healthiest diets in the world.

1 (28-ounce) can diced tomatoes with basil, garlic, and oregano

2 (15-ounce) cans cannellini beans, drained and rinsed

¼ cup diced green olives

½ cup vegetable broth

1 teaspoon extra-virgin olive oil or 1 tablespoon vegetable broth or water

4 teaspoons minced garlic (about 4 cloves)

10 ounces arugula

½ cup lemon juice (about 4 small lemons)

1.   In a large saucepan or soup pot, bring the tomatoes with their juices, beans, olives, and broth to a boil. Reduce the heat and simmer for about 10 minutes.

2.   Meanwhile, in a large skillet over medium-high heat, heat the olive oil. Add the garlic and sauté until it begins to brown, about 5 minutes. Add the arugula and lemon juice. Stir, cover, and reduce the heat to low. Steam for 3 minutes.

3.   Divide the arugula evenly among 4 single-serving containers, then spoon the beans over the arugula. Let cool before sealing the lids.

Storage: Place the airtight containers in the refrigerator for 5 days or freeze for up to 2 months. Thaw in the refrigerator overnight, and reheat in the microwave for 2½ to 3 minutes or in a saucepan over medium heat for 10 minutes.

TIP: Switch this recipe up by alternating beans (try great northern or navy) and greens (spinach is excellent).

Per Serving: Calories: 310; Fat: 4g; Protein: 18g; Carbohydrates: 53g; Fiber: 18g; Sugar: 12g; Sodium: 810mg

CHEESY MUSHROOM POLENTA

MAKES 6 SERVINGS

Prep: 5 minutes / Cook: 25 minutes

This is a rich, nutrient-packed dish that you simply serve in a bowl. Spoon it over roasted or steamed vegetables for a heartier meal. This recipe is excellent with Dilly White Beans (page 106) and Garlic and Herb Zoodles (page 93).

4 cups vegetable broth

2 cups water

1¾ cups cornmeal

1 teaspoon salt

1 teaspoon ground cumin

½ teaspoon ground turmeric

1 teaspoon extra-virgin olive oil or vegan butter or ¼ cup vegetable broth

2 cups chopped mushrooms (white, baby bella, or shiitake)

¼ cup nutritional yeast

2 teaspoons vegan butter

1 tablespoon lemon juice (about ½ small lemon)

1. In a large saucepan or pot, bring the broth and water to a boil. Slowly whisk in the cornmeal. Stir in the salt, cumin, and turmeric. Reduce the heat to low and cook until it thickens and the cornmeal is tender, stirring often, about 15 minutes.

2. Meanwhile, in a medium saucepan over medium-high heat, heat the olive oil. Add the mushrooms and cook, stirring frequently, for 5 minutes. Set aside.

3. Remove the cooked polenta from the stove. Add the nutritional yeast, vegan butter, lemon juice, and cooked mushrooms. Mix well.

4. Divide the polenta evenly among 6 single-serving containers. Let cool before sealing the lids.

Storage: Place the airtight containers in the refrigerator for 1 week or freeze for up to 1 month. To thaw, refrigerate overnight. Reheat in the microwave for 2 minutes.

TIP: Pressure cooker and multicooker aficionados, combine the broth, water, cornmeal, salt, cumin, and turmeric in the pot. Set for 5 minutes at high pressure and use a natural release. Continue the recipe from step 2.

Per Serving: Calories: 174; Fat: 4g; Protein: 5g; Carbohydrates: 32g; Fiber: 4g; Sugar: 2g; Sodium: 572mg

TLT WRAP

Prep: 10 minutes / Cook: 15 minutes

The vegan version of a traditional BLT sandwich is often referred to as a TLT. The first *T* is for seasoned tempeh. This is a hearty sandwich, fun to make and easy to eat on the go!

1 cup water

1 pound tempeh

¼ cup maple syrup

2 teaspoons extra-virgin olive oil or canola oil

1 teaspoon vegan Worcestershire sauce or tamari or soy sauce

⅛ teaspoon liquid smoke

1 teaspoon ground cayenne pepper

Nonstick cooking spray

4 vegan tortillas (whole-wheat, flour, spinach, or gluten-free)

8 lettuce leaves (romaine, red leaf, or green leaf)

2 large tomatoes, cut into 8 slices total

½ cup vegan mayonnaise or Caesar-Style Dressing (page 117)

1. In a large pot, bring the water to a boil. Place a steam basket over the water, and add the tempeh. Cover and steam for 10 minutes. Remove and let cool before slicing into 16 strips.

2. In a small bowl, whisk together the maple syrup, olive oil, Worcestershire sauce, liquid smoke, and cayenne pepper.

3. Spray a large skillet with nonstick cooking spray and set over medium-high heat. Add the tempeh strips. Pour the sauce over the tempeh, and fry for about 6 minutes, turning after 3 minutes. Transfer the tempeh to a plate.

4. Assemble each wrap as follows: 1 tortilla, 2 lettuce leaves, 2 tomato slices, 4 strips of tempeh, and 2 tablespoons of vegan mayonnaise. Roll the tortillas up and seal each in a single-serving storage container or quart-size plastic bag.

Storage: Place the containers in the refrigerator for up to 1 week. Serve cold.

TIP: This recipe works great with tofu, too!

Per serving: Calories: 434; Fat: 23g; Protein: 23g; Carbohydrates: 41g; Fiber: 3g; Sugar: 15g; Sodium: 332mg

"BEEFY" BEAN CHILI

MAKES 4 SERVINGS

Prep: 10 minutes / Cook: 30 minutes

New vegans often like to make foods that are familiar. Add a wholesome soy product, like textured vegetable protein, or TVP, and you get a ground beef–style chili that's 100 percent plant-based. Chili is always a great meal, but try it over Basic Baked Potatoes (page 99) and you'll thank me later.

1 cup textured vegetable protein (TVP)

1½ cups warm no-beef broth, divided

1 tablespoon extra-virgin olive oil or 2 tablespoons water

1 cup diced onion

3 teaspoons minced garlic (about 3 cloves)

1 teaspoon chipotle powder

1 teaspoon paprika

1 teaspoon chili powder

1 teaspoon ground cumin

½ teaspoon red pepper flakes

1 (14-ounce) can black beans, drained and rinsed, or 1½ cups cooked black beans

1 (14.5-ounce) can diced tomatoes

2 teaspoons tomato paste

1 to 2 tablespoons diced jalapeño pepper (optional)

½ to 1 teaspoon salt, to taste

¼ to ½ teaspoon freshly ground black pepper, to taste

1. In a small bowl, combine the TVP with 1 cup of warm broth. Let stand for 10 minutes to reconstitute.

2. In a large pot over medium-high heat, heat the olive oil. Add the onion and garlic and sauté for 5 minutes, until the onions are translucent. Add the chipotle powder, paprika, chili powder, cumin, red pepper flakes, and TVP. Stir well. Add the black beans, tomatoes, tomato paste, the remaining ½ cup of broth, jalapeño (if using), salt, and black pepper. Bring to a boil.

3. Cover, reduce the heat to low, and simmer for 20 minutes.

4. Divide the chili evenly among 4 single-serving storage containers or large glass jars. Let cool before sealing the lids.

Storage: Place the airtight containers in the refrigerator for up to 5 days or freeze for up to 3 months. To thaw, refrigerate overnight. To reheat, microwave for 2 to 3 minutes.

TIP: The brands Beyond Meat, Simple Truth, and Gardein all make vegan ground crumbles that can be found in the frozen-food section at the grocer.

Per Serving: Calories: 260; Fat: 5g; Protein: 23g; Carbohydrates: 35g; Fiber: 8g; Sugar: 4g; Sodium: 309mg

QUINOA PILAF

Prep: 10 minutes / Cook: 25 minutes

Quinoa is an "honorary legume," so when you make an easy recipe like this, you're getting quality protein and lots of vitamins and minerals. This pilaf is excellent with Miso Root Veggies (page 95).

1 cup dry quinoa

1 teaspoon extra-virgin olive oil or 2 teaspoons vegetable broth or water

½ cup chopped red onion

1 cup diced carrot

1½ cups vegetable broth

½ teaspoon dried parsley

½ teaspoon dried thyme

½ teaspoon salt

¼ to ½ cup chopped walnuts, to taste

1. In a mesh colander, rinse the quinoa.

2. In a large saucepan over medium-high heat, heat the olive oil. Combine the onion and carrot and sauté for 3 minutes. Add the broth, parsley, thyme, salt, and quinoa. Stir to combine. Bring to a boil. Cover, reduce the heat to low, and simmer for 15 to 20 minutes, until the broth is absorbed.

3. Remove from the stove and let stand for 5 minutes. Fluff before gently folding in the chopped walnuts.

4. Into each of 4 single-serving storage containers, spoon about 1 cup of quinoa. Let cool before sealing the lids.

Storage: Place the airtight containers in the refrigerator for up to 5 days or freeze for up to 3 months. To thaw, refrigerate overnight. Reheat in the microwave for 2 to 3 minutes.

TIP: Shake things up by opting for red quinoa and serving over bright greens for a plate inspired by the rainbow.

Per Serving: Calories: 202; Fat: 5g; Protein: 7g; Carbohydrates: 33g; Fiber: 5g; Sugar: 2g; Sodium: 355mg

COWBOY CAVIAR SALAD

MAKES 4 SERVINGS

Prep: 15 minutes

I suspect we all have that one recipe that we could always count on at a family gathering or community potluck. For my family it was "cowboy caviar." (Little did we know we were eating something that was oh-so vegan.) It's typically served as an appetizer with chips. Here we make it the star of a mason jar salad.

1 large tomato, diced

1 red bell pepper, diced

1 green bell pepper, diced

1 small red onion, diced

1 (14.5-ounce) can black-eyed peas, rinsed and drained

1 (14.5-ounce) can black beans, rinsed and drained

1 (14.5-ounce) can yellow corn, rinsed and drained

2 avocados, pitted

2 tablespoons lemon juice (about 1 small lemon)

¼ cup unseasoned rice vinegar, apple cider vinegar, or white wine vinegar

1 teaspoon dried oregano

½ teaspoon salt

8 cups loosely packed leafy greens (kale, spinach, arugula, or romaine lettuce), divided

1. In a large bowl, combine the tomato, peppers, onion, black-eyed peas, beans, and corn. Set aside.

2. In a blender, purée the avocados, lemon juice, vinegar, oregano, and salt to make a creamy dressing.

3. Into each of 4 wide-mouth quart jars, spoon about 2 tablespoons of the dressing. Add about 1¼ cups "caviar" followed by 2 cups of leafy greens to each. Seal the lids tightly.

Storage: Place the jars in the refrigerator for up to 1 week.

TIP: If you're prepping for just yourself, consider making only 2 salad jars and then using the remaining "caviar" for snacks this week; it's great on tortilla chips.

Per Serving: Calories: 411; Fat: 16g; Protein: 16g; Carbohydrates: 60g; Fiber: 19g; Sugar: 8g; Sodium: 543mg

QUINOA AND KALE BOWL

MAKES 4 SERVINGS

Prep: 5 minutes / Cook: 20 minutes

Quinoa and kale sound *so* vegan, don't they? Yep, because they are super healthy foods! This bowl is simple, yet flavorful and filling.

1 cup dry quinoa, rinsed

2 cups water

6 ounces kale, stemmed and chopped

1 small tomato, chopped

3 teaspoons lemon juice or 2 teaspoons unseasoned rice vinegar

¼ to ½ teaspoon salt (optional)

¼ teaspoon freshly ground black pepper

1. In a medium pot, combine the quinoa and water. Bring to a boil. Cover, reduce the heat to medium-low, and simmer for 15 to 20 minutes, until the water is absorbed.

2. Remove from the heat, add the kale to the pot (don't stir), and set aside for about 5 minutes. Add the tomato, lemon juice, salt (if using), and pepper and gently combine.

3. Into each of 4 single-serving storage containers, scoop 1 cup of quinoa. Let cool before sealing the lids.

Storage: Refrigerate for up to 5 days. Serve cold or reheat in the microwave for 1½ to 2 minutes. To freeze, place the containers in the freezer for up to 3 months. To thaw, refrigerate overnight. Serve cold or reheat in the microwave for 2 to 3 minutes.

TIP: To create a heartier meal, store in a wide-mouth pint jar and layer in these ingredients as follows: 2 tablespoons slivered almonds, ½ to 1 cup cooked quinoa and kale, and 1 cup arugula or spinach. Eat cold as a salad or reheat for 2 to 3 minutes.

Per Serving: Calories: 183; Fat: 3g; Protein: 8g; Carbohydrates: 33g; Fiber: 4g; Sugar: 1g; Sodium: 26mg

EASY KITCHARI

MAKES 5 SERVINGS

Prep: 20 minutes / Cook: 20 minutes

If you're looking for a comforting meal that is hearty and easy on the digestive system, this one's for you. A freezer staple in our house, it's my easy version of an Ayurveda kitchari recipe. To make it authentic, serve with fresh chopped cilantro and grated ginger root.

½ cup yellow mung beans or split peas

½ cup basmati rice

1 small red onion, diced

1 (14.5-ounce) can diced tomatoes

5 teaspoons minced garlic (about 5 cloves)

1 jalapeño, seeded

½ teaspoon ground ginger or 2 tablespoons minced fresh ginger

1 teaspoon ground turmeric

2 tablespoons to ¼ cup water

1 teaspoon extra-virgin olive oil or 1 to 2 tablespoons vegetable broth

1¼ teaspoons ground cumin

1¼ teaspoons ground coriander

1 teaspoon fennel seeds

4 cups chopped vegetables (mix of carrot, cauliflower, summer or winter squash, broccoli, and/or potatoes)

3 cups water

Juice of 1 large lemon

1 to 2 teaspoons salt, to taste

½ teaspoon freshly ground black pepper

1. Rinse and drain the beans and rice. Transfer to a small bowl and soak in water for 15 minutes.

2. In a food processor or blender, purée the onion, tomatoes with their juices, garlic, jalapeño, ginger, turmeric, and 2 tablespoons of water, adding water as necessary, until you reach a sauce consistency that pours easily and is not chunky.

3. In a large pot over medium-high heat, heat the olive oil. Add the cumin, coriander, and fennel seeds and sauté, stirring constantly, just until fragrant.

4. Transfer the purée to the pot.

5. Drain and rinse the soaked rice and beans, and add them to the pot. Add the chopped vegetables and water and combine well. Bring to a boil. Cover, reduce the heat to low, and simmer for 15 to 20 minutes, until the beans and rice are soft but not mushy. Add the lemon juice, and taste before adding the salt and pepper.

6. Into each of 5 single-serving storage containers, spoon 2 cups. Let cool before sealing.

Storage: Place the airtight containers in the refrigerator for up to 5 days or freeze for up to 3 months. To thaw, refrigerate overnight. Reheat for 3 to 3½ minutes in the microwave.

TIP: If you're looking for a nutritional "reboot," follow the Ayurveda tradition and eat this kitchari for all three meals for three days.

Per Serving: Calories: 234: Fat: 3g: Protein: 7g: Carbohydrates: 47g: Fiber: 13g: Sugar: 5g: Sodium: 862mg

ASIAN-INSPIRED CHILI

Prep: 15 minutes / Cook: 20 minutes

Here's another chili recipe, but this time with a nod to the East. Switching up flavor profiles is an easy way to avoid a culinary rut. This recipe uses a small bean—opt for red or adzuki—with savory seasonings often found in Japanese cuisine: cabbage, miso paste, and soy sauce. You can even give it a fiery, chili-like flavor by adding an Asian hot sauce, like yuzu or gochujang, or just grabbing whatever style hot sauce you keep in the pantry.

1 teaspoon sesame oil or 2 teaspoons vegetable broth or water

1 cup diced onion

3 teaspoons minced garlic (about 3 cloves)

1 cup chopped carrots

2 cups shredded green or napa cabbage

1 (14.5-ounce) can small red beans or adzuki beans, drained and rinsed

1 (14.5-ounce) fire-roasted diced tomatoes

2 cups vegetable broth

2 tablespoons red miso paste or tomato paste

2 tablespoons hot water

1 tablespoon hot sauce

2 teaspoons to 1 tablespoon tamari or soy sauce (optional)

1. In a large pot, over medium-high heat, heat the sesame oil. Add the onion, garlic, and carrot. Sauté for 5 minutes, until the onions are translucent. Add the cabbage, beans, tomatoes, and broth, and stir well. Bring to a boil.

2. Cover, reduce the heat to low, and simmer for 15 minutes.

3. In a measuring cup, whisk the miso paste and hot water. Set aside.

4. After 15 minutes, remove the chili from the stove, add the miso mixture and hot sauce, and stir well. Taste before determining how much tamari to add (if using).

5. Divide the chili evenly among 4 single-serving containers or large glass jars. Let cool before sealing the lids.

Storage: Place the containers in the refrigerator for up to 5 days or freeze for up to 3 months. To thaw, refrigerate overnight. Reheat in the microwave for 2 to 3 minutes.

TIP: If you opt for the adzuki beans and fall in love with the sweet legume as I have, make them a pantry staple and serve them heated up with Miso Spaghetti Squash (page 92) or Miso Root Veggies (page 95).

Per Serving: Calories: 177; Fat: 2g; Protein: 9g; Carbohydrates: 33g; Fiber: 11g; Sugar: 9g; Sodium: 764mg

Prep Seven

CUCUMBER AND ONION QUINOA SALAD

MAKES 4 SERVINGS

Prep: 15 minutes / Cook: 20 minutes

I grew up on summertime cucumbers and onions right out of the garden. My dad prepared them simply: sliced and in water, vinegar, and sugar. This variation recreates the flavor but becomes a meal, thanks to the quinoa.

1½ cups dry quinoa, rinsed and drained

2¼ cups water

⅓ cup white wine vinegar

2 tablespoons extra-virgin olive oil

1 tablespoon chopped fresh dill

1½ teaspoons vegan sugar

2 pinches salt

¼ teaspoon freshly ground black pepper

2 cups sliced sweet onions

2 cups diced cucumber

4 cups shredded lettuce

1.   In a medium pot, combine the quinoa and water. Bring to a boil. Cover, reduce the heat to medium-low, and simmer for 15 to 20 minutes, until the water is absorbed.

2.   Remove from the stove and let stand for 5 minutes.

3.   Fluff with a fork and set aside.

4.   Meanwhile, in a small bowl, mix the vinegar, olive oil, dill, sugar, salt, and pepper. Set aside.

5.   Into each of 4 wide-mouth jars, add 2 tablespoons of dressing, ½ cup of onions, ½ cup of cucumber, 1 cup of cooked quinoa, and 1 cup of shredded lettuce. Seal the lids tightly.

Storage: Place the airtight jars in the refrigerator for up to 5 days. To serve, shake and eat out of the jar or transfer to a bowl.

TIP: For an elevated flavor and appearance, use shredded endive or radicchio.

Per Serving: Calories: 369; Fat: 11g; Protein: 10g; Carbohydrates: 58g; Fiber: 6g; Sugar: 12g; Sodium: 88mg

HEALTHY MAC 'N' CHEESE

MAKES 4 SERVINGS

Prep: 5 minutes / Cook: 15 minutes

This recipe is basic on purpose. It's excellent as is, but consider prepping it in a jar. Start by adding 1 cup of frozen, canned, or fresh vegetables or even 1 or 2 cups of leafy greens, like arugula. Add the mac 'n' cheese and store. When you reheat, you'll have a full, balanced meal.

Salt for salting water, plus
½ teaspoon

8 ounces vegan elbow
macaroni

2 teaspoons minced garlic
(about 2 cloves)

2 tablespoons
nutritional yeast

2 teaspoons lemon juice
(about ½ small lemon)

1.   Bring a large pot of salted water to a boil. Cook the pasta according to the package directions, usually from 7 to 9 minutes. Once cooked, drain, and return the pasta to the pot.

2.   Add the garlic, nutritional yeast, lemon juice, and salt. Stir and combine well.

3.   Divide the mac and cheese evenly among 4 wide-mouth glass jars or single-serving containers. Let cool before sealing the lids.

Storage: Place the airtight containers in the refrigerator for up to 1 week or freeze for up to 2 months. To thaw, refrigerate overnight. Reheat in the microwave for 2 to 3 minutes.

TIPS: Boil the pasta in vegetable broth (or no-chicken broth) for an added boost of flavor. Buy quinoa vegan elbow macaroni for a gluten-free dish.

Per Serving: Calories: 232; Fat: 1g; Protein: 10g; Carbohydrates: 45g; Fiber: 3g; Sugar: 2g; Sodium: 298mg

CHICKPEA AND ARTICHOKE CURRY

MAKES 4 SERVINGS

Prep: 10 minutes / Cook: 15 minutes

If you want to ease into cooking foods from other regions, this curry is a great starter. Chickpeas and artichokes are easy to find, and you're going to use just a little curry and coconut milk. I think you'll like this texture and flavor. Serve it over steamed kale, spinach, or Swiss chard for a gorgeous bowl meal.

1 teaspoon extra-virgin olive oil or 2 teaspoons vegetable broth

1 small onion, diced

2 teaspoons minced garlic (2 cloves)

1 (14.5-ounce) can chickpeas, rinsed and drained

1 (14.5-ounce) can artichoke hearts, drained and quartered

2 teaspoons curry powder

½ teaspoon ground coriander

½ teaspoon ground cumin

1 (5.4-ounce) can unsweetened coconut milk

1. In a large skillet or pot over medium-high heat, heat the olive oil. Add the onion and garlic and sauté for about 5 minutes.

2. Add the chickpeas, artichoke hearts, curry powder, corian- der, and cumin. Stir to combine well. Pour the coconut milk into the pot, mix well, and bring to a boil. Cover, reduce the heat to low, and simmer for 10 minutes.

3. Divide the curry evenly among 4 wide-mouth glass jars or single-compartment containers. Let cool before sealing the lids.

Storage: Place the containers in the refrigerator for up to 5 days or freeze for up to 2 months. To thaw, refrigerate over- night. Reheat for 1½ to 3 minutes in the microwave.

TIP: I recommend storing this in wide-mouth pint jars because you can add as much baby spinach to the jars as they can hold. When you reheat in the microwave, the spinach will gently wilt. Turn the contents over in a bowl and voilà, a verdant, balanced meal.

Per Serving: Calories: 267; Fat: 12g; Protein: 9g; Carbohydrates: 36g; Fiber: 11g; Sugar: 3g; Sodium: 373mg

VEGETABLES

◀◀ Miso Root Veggies (page 95)

STEAMED CAULIFLOWER

Prep: 5 minutes / Cook: 10 minutes

Steamed vegetables are going to be your meal-prep friend. The trick is to not over-cook during preparation because you'll be reheating later, and no one wants mushy vegetables! Red pepper flakes are completely optional, but give it a try—it's such an easy way to give a simple veggie a flavor boost!

1 large head cauliflower

1 cup water

½ teaspoon salt

1 teaspoon red pepper flakes (optional)

1.   Remove any leaves from the cauliflower, and cut it into florets.

2.   In a large saucepan, bring the water to a boil. Place a steamer basket over the water, and add the florets and salt. Cover and steam for 5 to 7 minutes, until tender.

3.   In a large bowl, toss the cauliflower with the red pepper flakes (if using).

4.   Transfer the florets to a large airtight container or 6 single-serving containers. Let cool before sealing the lids.

Storage: Place the airtight containers in the refrigerator for up to 1 week or freeze for up to 6 months. To thaw, refrigerate overnight. Reheat in the microwave for 2 to 3 minutes.

> **TIP:** Transfer the steamed cauliflower to a food processor and chop for just 10 to 15 seconds to create a vegetable-based "rice."

Per Serving: Calories: 35; Fat: 0g; Protein: 3g; Carbohydrates: 7g; Fiber: 4g; Sugar: 4g; Sodium: 236mg

CAJUN SWEET POTATOES

Prep: 5 minutes / Cook: 30 minutes

Roasting vegetables is one of the easiest vegan cooking techniques but one I think some skip simply because of the perceived amount of time. Dice or cube root vegetables into small bites as we do here with the sweet potatoes, and you'll be enjoying comforting, healthy vegetables in no time.

2 pounds sweet potatoes

2 teaspoons extra-virgin olive oil

½ teaspoon ground cayenne pepper

½ teaspoon smoked paprika

½ teaspoon dried oregano

½ teaspoon dried thyme

½ teaspoon garlic powder

½ teaspoon salt (optional)

1. Preheat the oven to 400°F. Line a baking sheet with parchment paper.

2. Wash the potatoes, pat dry, and cut into ¾-inch cubes. Transfer to a large bowl, and pour the olive oil over the potatoes.

3. In a small bowl, combine the cayenne, paprika, oregano, thyme, and garlic powder. Sprinkle the spices over the potatoes and combine until the potatoes are well coated.

4. Spread the potatoes on the prepared baking sheet in a single layer. Season with the salt (if using). Roast for 30 minutes, stirring the potatoes after 15 minutes.

5. Divide the potatoes evenly among 4 single-serving containers. Let cool completely before sealing.

Storage: Place the containers in the refrigerator for up to 1 week. To heat, microwave for 1½ to 2 minutes.

TIP: Leftover cold roasted root vegetables are delicious in a salad. Try it!

Per Serving: Calories: 219; Fat: 3g; Protein: 4g; Carbohydrates: 46g; Fiber: 7g; Sugar: 9g; Sodium: 125mg

MISO SPAGHETTI SQUASH

MAKES 4 SERVINGS

Prep: 5 minutes / Cook: 40 minutes

Here's another low-carb replacement for traditional pasta, though I find myself simply using it as a delicious side dish or the top layer of a Buddha bowl of beans and grains. Try adding it to soup!

1 (3-pound) spaghetti squash

1 tablespoon hot water

1 tablespoon unseasoned rice vinegar

1 tablespoon white miso

1. Preheat the oven to 400°F. Line a rimmed baking sheet with parchment paper.

2. Halve the squash lengthwise and place, cut-side down, on the prepared baking sheet. Bake for 35 to 40 minutes, until tender.

3. Cool until the squash is easy to handle. With a fork, scrape out the flesh, which will be stringy, like spaghetti. Transfer to a large bowl.

4. In a small bowl, combine the hot water, vinegar, and miso with a whisk or fork. Pour over the squash. Gently toss with tongs to coat the squash.

5. Divide the squash evenly among 4 single-serving containers. Let cool before sealing the lids.

Storage: Place in the refrigerator for up to 1 week or freeze for up to 4 months. To thaw, refrigerate overnight. Reheat in a microwave for 2 to 3 minutes.

TIP: You can opt for a speedier squash by using an Instant Pot. Place the squash in a steam basket or on a trivet over ½ cup of water in the pot. Cook on high pressure for 15 minutes; use a natural release.

Per Serving: Calories: 117; Fat: 2g; Protein: 3g; Carbohydrates: 25g; Fiber: 0g; Sugar: 0g; Sodium: 218mg

GARLIC AND HERB ZOODLES

Prep: 5 to 10 minutes / Cook: 2 minutes

This is a zesty version of the low-carb-diet darling zucchini noodles. Note that the cooking time is super quick because you'll be reheating them later, and you don't want mushy zoodles. If you like raw zoodles, simply combine all the ingredients in a bowl and transfer to a large container or four wide-mouth jars to layer with ingredients for a salad in jar.

1 teaspoon extra-virgin olive oil or 2 tablespoons vegetable broth

1 teaspoon minced garlic (about 1 clove)

4 medium zucchini, spiralized

½ teaspoon dried basil

½ teaspoon dried oregano

¼ to ½ teaspoon red pepper flakes, to taste

¼ teaspoon salt (optional)

¼ teaspoon freshly ground black pepper

1.   In a large skillet over medium-high heat, heat the olive oil. Add the garlic, zucchini, basil, oregano, red pepper flakes, salt (if using), and black pepper. Sauté for 1 to 2 minutes, until barely tender.

2.   Divide the zoodles evenly among 4 storage containers. Let cool before sealing the lids.

Storage: Place the airtight containers in the refrigerator for up to 1 week. To reheat, microwave for 1½ to 2 minutes.

TIPS: You can make zoodles without a spiralizer! Try a vegetable peeler to make long, fettuccini-style zucchini strips or simply use a knife and make long, thicker strips. Cook for 2 to 3 minutes if using this technique.

Per Serving: Calories: 44: Fat: 2g: Protein: 3g: Carbohydrates: 7g: Fiber: 2g: Sugar: 3g: Sodium: 20mg

SMOKY COLESLAW

Prep: 10 minutes

I adore this recipe because it's the perfect dish to take to a party or holiday meal. It's a "familiar" food, and so easy to make vegan. But I love it even more for meal preps because it can serve as the base of a salad jar or can be served on tacos, tostadas, or even vegan hot dogs or shredded jackfruit sandwiches.

1 pound shredded cabbage

⅓ cup vegan mayonnaise

¼ cup unseasoned
   rice vinegar

3 tablespoons plain vegan
   yogurt or plain soymilk

1 tablespoon vegan sugar

½ teaspoon salt

¼ teaspoon freshly ground
   black pepper

¼ teaspoon smoked paprika

¼ teaspoon chipotle powder

1. Put the shredded cabbage in a large bowl.

2. In a medium bowl, whisk the mayonnaise, vinegar, yogurt, sugar, salt, pepper, paprika, and chipotle powder. Pour over the cabbage, and mix with a spoon or spatula and until the cabbage shreds are coated.

3. Divide the coleslaw evenly among 6 single-serving containers. Seal the lids.

Storage: Place the airtight containers in the refrigerator for 1 week.

TIP: Dulse (a seaweed) flakes are a great salt substitute; use 2 teaspoons of dulse flakes per ½ teaspoon of salt.

Per Serving: Calories: 73; Fat: 4g; Protein: 1g; Carbohydrates: 8g; Fiber: 2g; Sugar: 5g; Sodium: 283mg

MISO ROOT VEGGIES

Prep: 10 minutes / Cook: 40 minutes

Noticing a theme with the Asian-inspired flavors? I took a macrobiotic cooking class early on as a new vegan, and it's there where I learned how simply using unseasoned rice vinegar and low-sodium tamari or soy sauce can add depth to simple soup and bean recipes. And, yes, even straightforward vegetables.

Nonstick cooking spray (optional)

8 ounces carrots (about 2 large)

8 ounces beets

8 ounces parsnip (about 2 medium)

8 ounces sweet potatoes

2 tablespoons white or red miso paste

2 tablespoons unseasoned rice vinegar

2 tablespoons tamari or soy sauce

1. Preheat the oven to 425°F. Spray a rimmed baking sheet with nonstick cooking spray (if using) or line it with parchment paper.

2. Wash and dice the carrots, beets, parsnips, and sweet potatoes into ½-inch cubes. Combine in a large mixing bowl.

3. In a small bowl, whisk together the miso paste, vinegar, and tamari. Pour the sauce over the vegetables and toss to coat. Transfer to the baking sheet, and spray nonstick cooking spray (if using) over the vegetables. Roast for 30 to 40 minutes, until tender.

4. Divide the vegetables evenly among 4 single-serving containers. Let cool before sealing the lids.

Storage: Place the containers in the refrigerator for up to 1 week. To reheat, microwave for 1½ to 2 minutes or heat for 10 minutes in a toaster oven set to 350°F.

TIP: Roasted vegetables out of the oven are amazing, right? Well, reheated they are great, too, but don't expect the same texture. I love mixing roasted vegetables with Garlic and Herb Zoodles (page 93), Miso Spaghetti Squash (page 92), and Peppered Pinto Beans (page 102).

Per Serving: Calories: 185; Fat: 1g; Protein: 4g; Carbohydrates: 40g; Fiber: 7g; Sugar: 11g; Sodium: 688mg

CARAMELIZED ONION AND BEET SALAD

MAKES 4 SERVINGS

Prep: 10 minutes / Cook: 40 minutes

At first glance, this recipe may seem a little fussy. But read through it well—you're really just steaming a vegetable, and while it's steaming, you're cooking onions. Together, the result is an earthy, rich flavor that can add depth to a grain dish or simple salad.

3 medium golden beets

2 cups sliced sweet or Vidalia onions

1 teaspoon extra-virgin olive oil or no-beef broth

Pinch baking soda

¼ to ½ teaspoon salt, to taste

2 tablespoons unseasoned rice vinegar, white wine vinegar, or balsamic vinegar

1. Cut the greens off the beets, and scrub the beets. In a large pot, place a steamer basket and fill the pot with 2 inches of water. Add the beets, bring to a boil, then reduce the heat to medium, cover, and steam for about 35 minutes, until you can easily pierce the middle of the beets with a knife.

2. Meanwhile, in a large, *dry* skillet over medium heat, sauté the onions for 5 minutes, stirring frequently. Add the olive oil and baking soda, and continuing cooking for 5 more minutes, stirring frequently. Stir in the salt to taste before removing from the heat. Transfer to a large bowl and set aside.

3. When the beets have cooked through, drain and cool until easy to handle. Rub the beets in a paper towel to easily remove the skins. Cut into wedges, and transfer to the bowl with the onions. Drizzle the vinegar over everything and toss well.

4. Divide the beets evenly among 4 wide-mouth jars or storage containers. Let cool before sealing the lids.

Storage: Place the airtight containers in the refrigerator for up to 1 week or freeze for up to 3 months. To thaw, refrigerate overnight. Serve cold or heat in the microwave for 1½ to 3 minutes.

TIP: Cold beets are delicious in a salad jar. Turn these into a prep by layering the cooled beet salad over 2 tablespoons Tamari Almonds, (page 130), then filling the rest of the way with arugula, spinach, or red leaf lettuce. Store in the refrigerator for up to 1 week.

Per Serving: Calories: 104; Fat: 2g; Protein: 3g; Carbohydrates: 20g; Fiber: 4g; Sugar: 14g; Sodium: 303mg

SPICY FRUIT AND VEGGIE GAZPACHO

MAKES 8 SERVINGS

Prep: 10 minutes

Gazpacho is a great way to eat a raw meal packed with a variety of vegetables, and in this case, fruit, too. It's an ideal warm-weather starter or side dish, but consider adding a little "tofu feta" (see the tip) to make it a meal.

2 large tomatoes

1 serrano chile, seeded

4 cups cubed fresh watermelon, divided

2 teaspoons unseasoned rice vinegar or white wine vinegar

¼ cup extra-virgin olive oil or 2 to 3 tablespoons vegetable broth

1 large cucumber, peeled, seeded, and diced

1 small red onion, diced

1 small red bell pepper, seeded and diced

¼ cup minced fresh dill

Salt

Freshly ground black pepper

1. In a blender, purée the tomatoes, chile, and 2 cups of watermelon.

2. Pour in the vinegar and olive oil and pulse. Add the cucumber, onion, bell pepper, and dill and purée until smooth. Taste before seasoning with salt and black pepper.

3. In a large bowl, pour the gazpacho over the remaining 2 cups of watermelon.

4. Scoop 1½ cups of gazpacho into each of 8 single-serving containers. Seal the lids.

Storage: Place the airtight containers in the refrigerator for up to 1 week.

TIP: Bulk this soup up by adding "tofu feta." Combine 1 cup crumbled extra-firm tofu with 2 teaspoons lemon juice, 2 teaspoons unseasoned rice vinegar, 1 teaspoon nutritional yeast, 1 teaspoon white miso, ¼ teaspoon dried basil, ¼ teaspoon dried oregano, and a pinch or two of salt. Spoon 2 tablespoons over each serving.

Per Serving: Calories: 106; Fat: 7g; Protein: 2g; Carbohydrates: 12g; Fiber: 2g; Sugar: 8g; Sodium: 28mg

BAKED BRUSSELS SPROUTS

Prep: 10 minutes / Cook: 40 minutes

This one is for the Brussels sprouts lovers: simple seasonings, simple technique, simply tasty. Baked Brussels sprouts are great as a side dish, but I love using them as the green in a "beans, greens, and grains" bowl to shake up the typical steamed vegetable or leafy green.

1 pound Brussels sprouts

2 teaspoons extra-virgin olive or canola oil

4 teaspoons minced garlic (about 4 cloves)

1 teaspoon dried oregano

½ teaspoon dried rosemary

½ teaspoon salt

¼ teaspoon freshly ground black pepper

1 tablespoon balsamic vinegar

1. Preheat the oven to 400°F. Line a rimmed baking sheet with parchment paper.

2. Trim and halve the Brussels sprouts. Transfer to a large bowl. Toss with the olive oil, garlic, oregano, rosemary, salt, and pepper to coat well.

3. Transfer to the prepared baking sheet. Bake for 35 to 40 minutes, shaking the pan occasionally to help with even browning, until crisp on the outside and tender on the inside.

4. Remove from the oven and transfer to a large bowl. Stir in the balsamic vinegar, coating well.

5. Divide the Brussels sprouts evenly among 4 single-serving containers. Let cool before sealing the lids.

Storage: Place the airtight containers in the refrigerator for up to 1 week or freeze for up to 6 months. To thaw, refrigerate overnight. Reheat in the microwave for 1½ to 2 minutes.

TIP: If you have an air fryer, you can take these Brussels from frozen to "fried" in 7 minutes! Reheat in the air fryer on 390°F.

Per Serving: Calories: 77; Fat: 3g; Protein: 4g; Carbohydrates: 12g; Fiber: 5g; Sugar: 3g; Sodium: 320mg

BASIC BAKED POTATOES

MAKES 5 POTATOES

Prep: 5 minutes / Cook: 1 hour

Including a baked potato recipe in this book may seem, well, basic, but many people want to quickly reference the basics, and particularly when it comes to meal prep. Keep in mind that freezing potatoes isn't advised, so prepare the number of potatoes you think you'll consume over the week. Don't limit yourself to one type of potato! Bake two Russets, two yams, and a sweet potato to add variety to your preps throughout the week.

5 medium Russet potatoes or a variety of potatoes, washed and patted dry

1 to 2 tablespoons extra-virgin olive oil or aquafaba (see tip)

¼ teaspoon salt

¼ teaspoon freshly ground black pepper

1. Preheat the oven to 400°F.

2. Pierce each potato several times with a fork or a knife. Brush the olive oil over the potatoes, then rub each with a pinch of the salt and a pinch of the pepper. Place the potatoes on a baking sheet and bake for 50 to 60 minutes, until tender.

3. Place the potatoes on a baking rack and cool completely. Transfer to an airtight container or 5 single-serving containers. Let cool before sealing the lids.

Storage: Refrigerate for up to 1 week. To reheat, microwave for 2 to 3 minutes. Alternatively, set out and allow to come to room temperature. Preheat the oven to 450°F, and bake for about 10 minutes.

TIP: Aquafaba is the brine (broth) found in canned chickpeas. It's an oil-free alternative ideal for preparing crispy, golden, or browned foods.

Per Serving: Calories: 171; Fat: 3g; Protein: 4g; Carbohydrates: 34g; Fiber: 5g; Sugar: 3g; Sodium: 129mg

GRAINS AND BEANS

« Peppered Pinto Beans (page 102)

PEPPERED PINTO BEANS

MAKES 6 SERVINGS

Prep: 5 minutes / Cook: 20 minutes

Pinto beans are incredibly versatile. They are excellent in soup and chili, make a great base for baked beans, and are the star of refried beans. But with a fiery boost from fresh peppers, they stand up well on their own. Enjoy these with Spanish Rice (page 110) and steamed kale or spinach.

1 teaspoon extra-virgin olive oil or ¼ cup vegetable broth

1 red bell pepper, seeded and diced

1 jalapeño seeded and minced

2 (14.5-ounce) cans pinto beans, rinsed and drained

½ cup vegetable broth

1 teaspoon ground cumin

1 teaspoon chili powder

½ teaspoon salt (optional)

¼ teaspoon freshly ground black pepper

1.   In a large pot over medium-high heat, heat the olive oil. Sauté the bell pepper and jalapeño for 3 to 5 minutes. Add the beans, broth, cumin, chili powder, salt, and black pepper. Bring to a boil. Reduce the heat to low and simmer, uncovered, for 10 minutes.

2.   Transfer to a large storage container, or scoop about ⅓ cup of beans into each of 6 storage containers. Let cool before sealing the lids.

Storage: Place the airtight containers in the refrigerator for up to 5 days or freeze for up to 3 months. To thaw, refrigerate overnight. Reheat in the microwave for 1½ to 3 minutes.

TIP: Make quick refried beans by reheating in a small saucepan on the stove and adding a splash or two of vegetable broth while mashing with a potato masher.

Per Serving: Calories: 183; Fat: 2g; Protein: 11g; Carbohydrates: 32g; Fiber: 11g; Sugar: 2g; Sodium: 340mg

ITALIAN LENTILS

MAKES 6 SERVINGS

Prep: 5 minutes / Cook: 40 minutes

Rich in iron, dried lentils are one of the fastest-cooking legumes. Keeping cooked lentils ready in the refrigerator or freezer helps you pull together protein-rich meals in no time. They are perfect to add to soups and salads, to use as taco or wrap filling, or puréed for a bean dip. While we're using Italian-style herbs here, you can easily switch up the flavor profile with curry for Indian style or peppers for Mexican style. Please note that we're not using salt in this base recipe. Hold off on sodium seasoning until you know how you will use the lentils.

5 cups water

2¼ cups dry French or brown lentils, rinsed and drained

3 teaspoons minced garlic (about 3 cloves)

1 bay leaf

½ teaspoon dried basil

½ teaspoon dried oregano

½ teaspoon dried rosemary

½ teaspoon dried thyme

1. In a large pot, combine the water, lentils, garlic, bay leaf, basil, oregano, rosemary, and thyme. Bring to a boil.

2. Reduce the heat to low, cover, and simmer for 25 to 40 minutes, until tender, stirring occasionally.

3. Drain any excess cooking liquid.

4. Transfer to a large storage container, or scoop 1 cup of lentils into each of 6 storage containers. Let cool before sealing the lids.

Storage: Place the airtight containers in the refrigerator for up to 5 days or freeze for up to 3 months. To thaw, refrigerate overnight. Reheat in the microwave for 1½ to 3 minutes.

INGREDIENT TIP: For a little extra flavor, use vegetable broth either in place of all 5 cups of water or in a mix of 2½ cups water and 2½ cups vegetable broth.

MAKE IT FASTER: If you have a pressure cooker or multicooker, like an Instant Pot, combine all the ingredients in the pot and pressure cook for 8 to 10 minutes on high. Let the pressure release naturally.

Per Serving (1 cup): Calories: 257; Fat: 1g; Protein: 19g; Carbohydrates: 44g; Fiber: 22g; Sugar: 2g; Sodium: 5mg

RED PEPPER LENTILS

MAKES 4 SERVINGS

Prep: 5 minutes / Cook: 20 minutes

Red is the name of the game in this versatile legume recipe! Red lentils, unlike their brown and green cousins, actually get a bit mushy—in a good way—when cooked (think split peas). As a result, you can use these as a traditional bean dish and serve with a grain and vegetable, and you can also mash them with a potato masher (or purée them in a food processor) to turn it into more of a dip (think Indian-style dal).

1 teaspoon extra-virgin olive oil or canola oil or 2 teaspoons water or vegetable broth

2 teaspoons minced garlic (about 2 cloves)

2 teaspoons grated fresh ginger

½ teaspoon ground cumin

½ teaspoon fennel seeds

1 large red bell pepper, seeded and chopped

1 large tomato, chopped

1 cup dried red lentils

2¼ cups water

2 tablespoons lemon juice (about 1 small lemon)

1. In a large pot over medium-high heat, heat the olive oil. Add the garlic and ginger and sauté for 3 minutes, stirring frequently to keep the garlic from sticking. Add the cumin, fennel, red bell pepper, tomato, lentils, and water. Bring to a boil, cover, and reduce the heat to medium-low or low to simmer until the lentils are tender, about 15 minutes.

2. Remove from the heat, and stir in the lemon juice.

3. Transfer to a large storage container, or scoop ½ cup of lentils into each of 4 storage containers. Let cool before sealing the lids.

Storage: Place the airtight containers in the refrigerator for up to 5 days or freeze for up to 3 months. To thaw, refrigerate overnight. Reheat in the microwave for 1½ to 3 minutes.

TIP: Substitute these lentils for the hummus in Veggie Hummus Pinwheels (page 133).

Per Serving: Calories: 206; Fat: 2g; Protein: 13g; Carbohydrates: 34g; Fiber: 16g; Sugar: 4g; Sodium: 9mg

BALSAMIC BLACK BEANS

MAKES 5 SERVINGS

Prep: 5 minutes / Cook: 20 minutes

Vinegar is an umami ingredient that brings out the "meatiness" in plant-based cooking. Balsamic vinegar adds a sharp sweetness that elevates everyday black beans. Switch this recipe up any time by using other vinegars (red wine vinegar is excellent, too) and spices (try dill and garlic).

1 teaspoon extra-virgin olive oil or vegetable broth

½ cup diced sweet onion

1 teaspoon ground cumin

1 teaspoon ground cardamom (optional)

2 (14.5-ounce) cans black beans, rinsed and drained

¼ to ½ cup vegetable broth

2 tablespoons balsamic vinegar

1. In a large pot over medium-high heat, heat the olive oil. Add the onion, cumin, and cardamom (if using) and sauté for 3 to 5 minutes, until the onion is translucent. Add the beans and ¼ cup broth, and bring to a boil. Add up to ½ cup more of broth for "soupier" beans. Cover, reduce the heat, and simmer for 10 minutes.

2. Add the balsamic vinegar, increase the heat to medium-high, and cook for 3 more minutes uncovered.

3. Transfer to a large storage container, or divide the beans evenly among 5 single-serving storage containers. Let cool before sealing the lids.

Storage: Place the airtight containers in the refrigerator for up to 5 days or freeze for up to 2 months. To thaw, refrigerate overnight. Reheat in the microwave for 1½ to 3 minutes.

TIP: Store these flavorful black beans in a container with Garlic and Herb Zoodles (page 93) or over raw baby spinach.

Per Serving: Calories: 200: Fat: 2g; Protein: 13g; Carbohydrates: 34g; Fiber: 12g; Sugar: 1g; Sodium: 41mg

DILLY WHITE BEANS

Prep: 5 minutes / Cook: 20 minutes

White beans are a pantry staple for me because they make great dips and sauces (white bean gravy, anyone?). Great northern beans are perfect as a main dish because of their size and texture.

1 teaspoon extra-virgin olive oil or ¼ cup vegetable broth

1 small sweet onion, cut into half-moon slices

2 (14.5-ounce) cans great northern beans, rinsed and drained

½ cup vegetable broth

2 teaspoons dried dill

½ teaspoon salt (optional)

¼ teaspoon freshly ground black pepper

1. In a large skillet or wok over medium-high heat, heat the olive oil. Sauté the onion slices for 3 to 5 minutes, until the onion is translucent.

2. Add the beans, broth, dill, salt (if using), and pepper. Bring to a boil. Reduce the heat to low and simmer, uncovered, for 10 minutes.

3. Transfer to a large storage container, or scoop ½ cup of beans into each of 6 storage containers. Let cool before sealing the lids.

Storage: Place the airtight containers in the refrigerator for up to 5 days or freeze for up to 3 months. To thaw, refrigerate overnight. Reheat in the microwave for 1½ to 3 minutes.

TIP: Did you know you can cook canned beans in a pressure cooker or multicooker, like the Instant Pot? It doesn't actually make the process from start to finish faster, but you do get to set it and forget it (and the flavors will combine beautifully). Cook canned beans for 3 minutes on low pressure and use a quick release.

Per Serving: Calories: 155; Fat: 1g; Protein: 10g; Carbohydrates: 26g; Fiber: 9g; Sugar: 1g; Sodium: 67mg

SUSHI-STYLE QUINOA

Prep: 2 minutes / Cook: 25 minutes

Here we go: This is the first of several very easy grain recipes with an addition of a spice or seasoning that gives it a twist. I'm doing this because I want you to learn how to make vegan basics *and* I want you to flex your culinary muscles. Starting with quinoa, sushi style, we're adding umami savoriness to a simple grain (seed, actually). This is delicious combined in a mason jar with your favorite vegan sushi fillings (avocado, roasted sweet potatoes, red peppers, carrot sticks, etc.) and shredded nori sheets for a deconstructed vegan sushi salad jar.

2 cups water

1 cup dry quinoa, rinsed

¼ cup unseasoned rice vinegar

¼ cup mirin or white wine vinegar

1. In a large saucepan, bring the water to a boil.

2. Add the quinoa to the boiling water, stir, cover, and reduce the heat to low. Simmer for 15 to 20 minutes, until the liquid is absorbed. Remove from the heat and let stand for 5 minutes. Fluff with a fork. Add the vinegar and mirin, and stir to combine well.

3. Divide the quinoa evenly among 4 mason jars or single-serving containers. Let cool before sealing the lids.

Storage: Place the airtight containers in the refrigerator for up to 5 days or freeze for up to 2 months. To thaw, refrigerate overnight. Eat cold in salads or reheat in the microwave for 1½ to 3 minutes.

TIP: If you don't want to buy mirin or white wine vinegar, use ½ cup unseasoned rice vinegar and whisk 1 teaspoon agave syrup into it before adding it to the quinoa.

Per Serving: Calories: 192; Fat: 3g; Protein: 6g; Carbohydrates: 34g; Fiber: 3g; Sugar: 4g; Sodium: 132mg

FIVE-SPICE FARRO

MAKES 4 SERVINGS

Prep: 3 minutes / Cook: 35 minutes

Farro is a chewy grain that adds a depth of texture to salads and soups and even stands in great as a ground meat substitute. Low-fat, high-fiber, and rich in iron, it packs a nutritional punch. Five-spice powder, common in several Asian cuisines and some Middle Eastern cooking, adds a savory flavor.

1 cup dried farro, rinsed and drained

1 teaspoon five-spice powder

1. In a medium pot, combine the farro, five-spice powder, and enough water to cover. Bring to a boil; reduce the heat to medium-low, and simmer for 30 minutes. Drain off any excess water.

2. Transfer to a large storage container, or scoop 1 cup farro into each of 4 storage containers. Let cool before sealing the lids.

Storage: Place the airtight containers in the refrigerator for 1 week or freeze for up to 3 months. To thaw, refrigerate over-night. Reheat in the microwave for 1½ to 3 minutes.

INGREDIENT TIP: Make your own five-spice powder by simply combining ground star anise, ground cloves, ground cinnamon, freshly ground black or white pepper, and ground fennel seeds. Store in a shaker and use in place of salt and pepper.

PRESSURE COOKER TIP: Combine the farro, five-spice powder, and 3 cups water in the pot. Cover and cook at high pressure for 10 minutes. Use a natural release. Drain off any excess water.

Per Serving: Calories: 73; Fat: 0g; Protein: 3g; Carbohydrates: 15g; Fiber: 1g; Sugar: 0g; Sodium: 0mg

PESTO PEARLED BARLEY

MAKES 4 SERVINGS

Prep: 1 minute / Cook: 50 minutes

Barley is a chewy grain that adds a depth of texture to plates filled with beans and grains. The Italian grain, amped up with pesto, is ideal for Italian-style dishes. It's terrific with Dilly White Beans (page 106).

1 cup dried barley

2½ cups vegetable broth

½ cup Parm-y Kale Pesto (page 114)

1. In a medium saucepan, combine the barley and broth and bring to a boil. Cover, reduce the heat to low, and simmer for about 45 minutes, until tender. Remove from the stove and let stand for 5 minutes.

2. Fluff the barley, then gently fold in the pesto.

3. Scoop about ¾ cup into each of 4 single-compartment storage containers. Let cool before sealing the lids.

Storage: Place storage containers in the refrigerator for up to 5 days or freeze for up to 3 months. To thaw, refrigerate overnight. Reheat in the microwave for 1½ to 3 minutes.

TIP: Farro and wheat berries are excellent substitutes for barley.

Per Serving: Calories: 237; Fat: 6g; Protein: 9g; Carbohydrates: 40g; Fiber: 11g; Sugar: 2g; Sodium: 365mg

SPANISH RICE

Prep: 10 minutes / Cook: 1 hour

This is an easy way to make your brown rice a little more exciting. If you're a spice fan, consider adding a diced jalapeño! Serve with Peppered Pinto Beans (page 102) or Red Bean and Corn Salad (page 74).

1 teaspoon extra-virgin olive oil or 2 teaspoons vegetable broth

½ cup finely chopped onion

1 teaspoon minced garlic (about 1 clove)

1 cup short-grain brown rice

2¼ cups vegetable broth

2 teaspoons tomato paste

1 small tomato, diced

½ teaspoon ground cumin

½ teaspoon paprika

½ teaspoon chili powder

¼ teaspoon salt

1. In a large saucepan over medium-high, heat the olive oil. Sauté the onion and garlic for 3 to 5 minutes, until the onions are translucent. Add the rice and stir constantly, allowing the rice to brown just a bit. Add the broth, tomato paste, tomato, cumin, paprika, chili powder, and salt. Bring to a boil. Cover the pan, reduce the heat to low, and simmer for 45 minutes.

2. Remove from the heat but leave covered for 15 minutes. Fluff with a fork.

3. Divide the rice evenly among 4 single-compartment storage containers. Let cool before sealing the lids.

Storage: Place the airtight containers in the refrigerator for up to 1 week or freeze for up to 2 months. To thaw, refrigerate overnight. Reheat in the microwave for 1½ to 3 minutes.

TIP: Make this fast in your Instant Pot or pressure cooker! Sauté the onion, garlic, and rice in the pot as in the directions, add the rest of the ingredients (but decrease the vegetable broth to 1½ cups), and cook on high pressure for 22 minutes; use a natural release.

Per Serving: Calories: 161; Fat: 2g; Protein: 4g; Carbohydrates: 31g; Fiber: 3g; Sugar: 3g; Sodium: 324mg

BAKED WILD RICE

MAKES 4 SERVINGS

Prep: 5 minutes / Cook: 1 hour 10 minutes

This colorful recipe is great year-round but a real showstopper during the holidays. Note that we aren't focusing on spices here, just a good old-fashioned mirepoix (onion, carrots, and celery)—which makes this a perfect side for a flavor bomb entrée like Dilly White Beans (page 106).

1 tablespoon vegan butter or extra-virgin olive oil or 2 tablespoons water

1 cup chopped white or yellow onion

½ cup chopped carrot

½ cup chopped celery

1 cup chopped mushrooms

1½ cups wild rice

4 cups vegetable broth

1 cup chopped dried cranberries or cherries

½ cup chopped pistachios

1. Preheat the oven to 375°F.

2. In a Dutch oven with a lid or in a large, oven-safe skillet over medium-high heat, heat the vegan butter. Add the onion, carrot, and celery and sauté for 5 minutes. Add the mushrooms and sauté for 3 more minutes.

3. Stir in the rice and broth, mixing well. Cover with a lid or aluminum foil and bake for 30 minutes.

4. Remove the pan from the oven, uncover, and stir in the dried cranberries. Return to the oven uncovered and bake for 20 to 30 minutes longer, until the liquid is absorbed and the rice is tender.

5. Remove from the oven and stir in the pistachios.

6. Divide the rice evenly among 4 storage containers. Let cool before sealing the lids.

Storage: Place the airtight containers in the refrigerator for up to 1 week or freeze for up to 3 months. To thaw, refrigerate overnight. Reheat in the microwave for 1½ to 3 minutes.

TIP: Pistachios are considered an "honorary legume" because of their nutritional value and high protein content. Increase the pistachios to 1 cup to turn this baked side into the main course.

Per Serving: Calories: 355; Fat: 8g; Protein: 11g; Carbohydrates: 63g; Fiber: 7g; Sugar: 14g; Sodium: 496mg

SAUCES, DRESSINGS, AND DIPS

◀◀ Edamame Hummus (page 118)

PARM-Y KALE PESTO

MAKES 1 1/2 CUPS

Prep: 10 minutes

Pesto is great as a vegetable dip, sandwich spread, or garlic toast topping, and mixed with oil and vinegar, for a hearty salad dressing. Be sure to try it in Pesto Pearled Barley (page 109).

2 cups tightly packed kale, torn into bite-size pieces

¾ cup nutritional yeast

½ cup chopped walnuts

3 teaspoons minced garlic (about 3 cloves)

2 tablespoons lemon juice (about 1 small lemon)

¼ cup extra-virgin olive oil

⅛ teaspoon salt

⅛ teaspoon freshly ground black pepper

In a food processor or blender, process the kale, nutritional yeast, walnuts, garlic, lemon juice, olive oil, salt, and pepper until well mixed, but with just a bit of rough texture. Transfer to a wide-mouth pint jar and close tightly with a lid.

Storage: Place the airtight jar in the refrigerator for up to 2 weeks or freeze for up to 2 months. To thaw, refrigerate overnight.

TIP: Turn Taco Pita Pizzas (page 128) into an Italian-style snack. Use this pesto as a substitute for the refried beans.

Per Serving (½ cup): Calories: 286; Fat: 22g; Protein: 13g; Carbohydrates: 16g; Fiber: 7g; Sugar: 0g; Sodium: 125mg

WHITE BEAN AND SUN-DRIED TOMATO DIP

MAKES ABOUT 1 ½ CUPS

Prep: 5 minutes

This is another nod to the Mediterranean diet. The bonus here is that the sun-dried tomatoes add umami (plant-sourced "meatiness"!) and lots of great nutrients, including protein, fiber, potassium, and B vitamins. This dip is great with raw vegetables or crackers or wrapped up in a sandwich. Try a dollop over chopped lettuce for a quick, protein-rich salad.

1 (14.5-ounce) can cannellini beans, rinsed and drained

⅓ cup oil-packed sun-dried tomatoes

1 to 2 teaspoons minced garlic (about 1 to 2 cloves), to taste

Large pinch salt

1 to 2 tablespoons lemon juice (about ½ to 1 small lemon), to taste

In a food processor or high-speed blender, combine the beans, sun-dried tomatoes, garlic, and salt. Pulse until coarsely chopped. With the food processor running, slowly drizzle lemon juice in until the dip is creamy. Transfer to a wide-mouth pint jar and close tightly with a lid.

Storage: Place the airtight jar in the refrigerator for up to 5 days.

TIP: Any bean will do! Try making this dip with chickpeas or black beans.

Per Serving (½ cup): Calories: 286: Fat: 11g: Protein: 9g: Carbohydrates: 39g: Fiber: 11g: Sugar: 9g: Sodium: 462mg

CURRIED PEANUT BUTTER

MAKES 1½ CUPS

Prep: 15 minutes

Homemade peanut (or other nut) butter is so easy to make! In this recipe I use curry with a nod to global cuisine. Make an "adult PB&J" with this curry nut butter and mango chutney. You can change the flavor profile by swapping out the curry and using ½ teaspoon of your favorite spice or spice blend.

1½ cups raw, unsalted peanuts

¼ teaspoon salt

½ teaspoon curry powder

2 teaspoons extra-virgin olive oil, plus more if needed

1. In a food processor fitted with the S blade, process the peanuts for 6 minutes. At 6 minutes, scrape down the sides, add the salt, curry, and olive oil, and process for another 6 minutes. Add additional olive oil if the nut butter appears too dry.

2. Transfer to a wide-mouth pint jar and close tightly with a lid.

Storage: Place the airtight jar in the refrigerator for up to 1 month.

TIP: Turn this nut butter into a sauce! Blend a couple of tablespoons with a splash of almond milk to your desired consistency.

Per Serving (2 tablespoons): Calories: 110; Fat: 10g; Protein: 5g; Carbohydrates: 3g; Fiber: 2g; Sugar: 1g; Sodium: 42mg

CAESAR-STYLE DRESSING

MAKES ABOUT 1 ½ CUPS

Prep: 5 minutes

A classic made vegan. No eggs here, folks. Just umami-rich ingredients that bring out the taste we expect. If you're not a fan of jarred mayo, use a plain vegan yogurt instead.

3 tablespoons vegan mayonnaise

2 tablespoons vegan Worcestershire sauce

1 tablespoon Dijon mustard

1 teaspoon red wine vinegar

4 teaspoons minced garlic (about 4 cloves)

¾ cup extra-virgin olive oil

¼ cup nutritional yeast

¼ teaspoon salt

¼ teaspoon freshly ground black pepper

1. In a blender or food processor, combine the mayonnaise, Worcestershire, mustard, vinegar, and garlic. Blend until the ingredients are well combined. You might need to stop and scrape down the sides during this process to ensure all ingredients are mixed well.

2. With the blender running, slowly add the olive oil until the dressing begins to thicken. Continue to add olive oil until desired consistency. Add the nutritional yeast, and pulse a few times to incorporate. Season with the salt and pepper, and do a final pulse or two.

3. Transfer to a wide-mouth pint jar and close tightly with a lid.

Storage: Place the airtight jar in the refrigerator for up to 7 days.

TIP: You can mix finely chopped walnuts with the nutritional yeast to pull in the "Parmesan" flavor and texture commonly found in a nonvegan Caesar salad.

Per Serving (2 tablespoons): Calories: 127; Fat: 14g; Protein: 1g; Carbohydrates: 2g; Fiber: 0g; Sugar: 1g; Sodium: 131mg

EDAMAME HUMMUS

MAKES 3 CUPS

Prep: 10 minutes

This bright green "hummus" stars edamame—a young soybean—but follows the basic hummus formula: legume, citrus juice, and tahini. It's a fun alternative to traditional chickpea hummus, with a bit of a lighter texture, and serves beautifully in verdant spinach tortillas or in a leafy green wrap, such as lettuce or collard greens.

1 pound frozen shelled edamame, thawed

⅓ cup tahini

2 tablespoons grated fresh ginger

3 teaspoons minced garlic (about 3 cloves)

2 tablespoons lemon juice (about 1 small lemon)

1 teaspoon salt

1 tablespoon sesame oil (optional)

1. In a food processor or high-speed blender, purée the edamame, tahini, ginger, garlic, lemon juice, and salt until smooth. With the motor running, slowly drizzle in the sesame oil (if using) until creamy.

2. Transfer to a storage container and seal the lid.

Storage: Place the airtight container in the refrigerator for 5 days.

INGREDIENT TIP: You can easily substitute any type of legume. Use 1 (14.5-ounce) can of chickpeas, lentils, or black beans. Just rinse and drain before using.

OIL-FREE TIP: If omitting the sesame oil, increase the amount of lemon juice, substitute 1 teaspoon plain vegan yogurt, or drizzle in water until creamy.

Per Serving (½ cup): Calories: 178; Fat: 11g; Protein: 10g; Carbohydrates: 11g; Fiber: 4g; Sugar: 2g; Sodium: 412mg

VEGAN THOUSAND ISLAND

MAKES 2 CUPS

Prep: 10 minutes

When I first went vegan, my husband didn't join my lifestyle. We did come together, however, in the kitchen. He felt like it was his personal mission to create vegan versions of recipes we loved so we could enjoy them together. And that's where this recipe originated. This dressing is great on sandwiches, on salads, and even as a dip for vegetables and crackers.

1¼ cups vegan mayonnaise

2 tablespoons unsweetened almond milk or soymilk, plus more if needed

¼ cup ketchup

2 teaspoons vegan Worcestershire sauce

¼ teaspoon salt, plus more if needed

4 to 6 tablespoons sweet pickle relish, to taste

1. In a blender or food processor, combine the mayonnaise, milk, ketchup, Worcestershire sauce, and ¼ teaspoon salt. Pulse until smooth, about 30 seconds. Add more nut milk if you prefer a smoother consistency.

2. Transfer the dressing to a bowl. Stir in the relish, and add additional salt to taste.

3. Transfer to a wide-mouth pint jar and close tightly with a lid.

Storage: Place the airtight jar in the refrigerator for up to 1 week.

TIP: Want to lighten this dressing up? Use plain vegan yogurt in place of the vegan mayonnaise.

Per Serving (2 tablespoons): Calories: 96; Fat: 8g; Protein: 0g; Carbohydrates: 4g; Fiber: 0g; Sugar: 2g; Sodium: 237mg

WHITE BEAN GRAVY

MAKES 2 ½ CUPS

Prep: 5 minutes / Cook: 15 minutes

This is one of the very first recipes I created when I went vegan. I've used a variation in almost every one of my books because I think it's that essential. It's packed with umami flavor and provides an amazing creamy texture. I have a local culinary class student (Hi, Rita!) who comes to every holiday cooking class I teach just so she can have this gravy!

¼ cup vegan butter

3 teaspoons minced garlic (about 3 cloves)

½ cup diced yellow onion

⅛ teaspoon dried sage

⅛ teaspoon dried rosemary

⅛ teaspoon freshly ground black pepper

1¼ cups vegetable broth

¼ cup tamari or soy sauce

1 (14.5-ounce) can white beans (any variety), drained and rinsed

¼ cup nutritional yeast

1. In a small saucepan over medium-high heat, heat the vegan butter. Add the garlic and onion and sauté for about 5 minutes, until the onion is translucent. Add the sage, rosemary, and pepper, and mix well. Stir in the broth and soy sauce. Bring the mixture to a boil.

2. Add the beans. Use an immersion blender in the saucepan to blend the gravy for 20 to 30 seconds, or until smooth. Alternatively, carefully transfer the gravy to a blender and blend until smooth, then return the gravy to the saucepan.

3. Cover the saucepan, reduce the heat to medium, and cook for 5 minutes, stirring occasionally. Add the nutritional yeast, stir well, then cover the saucepan and simmer for 5 minutes longer, stirring as needed.

4. Transfer to a large glass jar or storage container. Let cool before sealing the lid.

Storage: Store the airtight jar in the refrigerator for up to 5 days. Reheat in the microwave for 1½ to 2 minutes or in a saucepan on the stove for 8 to 10 minutes.

TIP: Make this when you're making Mashed Potatoes and Kale with White Beans (page 70). Serve it over that piping bowl of veggies and you've got a full meal.

Per Serving (½ cup): Calories: 217: Fat: 10g; Protein: 9g; Carbohydrates: 25g; Fiber: 9g; Sugar: 2g; Sodium: 797mg

EASY MARINARA

Prep: 5 minutes / Cook: 20 minutes

Sure, it's easy to keep store-bought jars of pasta sauce in your pantry, but this recipe is pretty darn easy, too. You can even add lentils—red for creaminess or brown for meatiness—and turn it into a whole second and third sauce! Use it for dipping Risotto Bites (page 126), or serve it over Garlic and Herb Zoodles (page 93).

1 teaspoon extra-virgin olive oil or vegetable broth

4 to 6 teaspoons minced garlic (about 4 to 6 cloves), to taste

1 cup diced onion

1 (28-ounce) can crushed tomatoes

½ cup vegetable broth

1 teaspoon dried basil

1 teaspoon dried oregano

1 teaspoon dried parsley

1 teaspoon dried thyme

½ teaspoon red pepper flakes

½ teaspoon salt

½ teaspoon vegan sugar (optional)

¼ teaspoon freshly ground black pepper

1. In a large saucepan over medium-high heat, heat the olive oil, garlic, and onion until the onion is translucent, about 5 minutes. Add the tomatoes, broth, basil, oregano, parsley, thyme, red pepper flakes, salt, sugar (if using), and black pepper. **Cover**, reduce the heat to low, and simmer for 15 to 20 minutes.

2. Transfer to a large airtight storage container, or scoop 1 cup into each of 5 single-serving jars or containers. Let cool before sealing the lids.

Storage: Place the airtight containers in the refrigerator for up to 1 week or freeze for up to 3 months. To thaw, refrigerate overnight. Reheat in the microwave for 2 to 3 minutes.

> **TIP:** Pour ½ cup of this marinara over one serving of Healthy Mac 'n' Cheese before storing for a simple, casserole-style pasta meal prep.

Per Serving (1 cup): Calories: 90; Fat: 1g; Protein: 5g; Carbohydrates: 16g; Fiber: 6g; Sugar: 10g; Sodium: 470mg

CASHEW CREAM

MAKES 1 TO 1½ CUPS

Prep: 1 hour 5 minutes

Cashew cream is one of those things that every vegan will eventually make. It's perfect over hot bowls of greens, as dressing on a salad, and drizzled over greens in a wrap. Try it on Veggie Hummus Pinwheels (page 133). Savory is almost always the name of the game for me, but be sure to check out my tip for a sweet cream!

1 cup raw cashews

2½ cups water, divided

2 tablespoons lemon juice (about 1 small lemon)

½ teaspoon salt

½ teaspoon unseasoned rice vinegar or apple cider vinegar

2 teaspoons minced garlic (about 2 cloves)

1 teaspoon smoked paprika (optional)

1 tablespoon extra-virgin olive oil

1. In a small bowl, soak the raw cashews in 2 cups of water for 1 hour. Rinse and drain.

2. Transfer the cashews to a blender, and add the lemon juice, salt, vinegar, garlic, and paprika. Blend at high speed, and slowly drizzle the olive oil into the mixture. If needed, slowly drizzle in the remaining ½ cup of water until you reach a thick, creamy consistency.

3. Transfer the cream into a glass jar. Close the lid tightly.

Storage: Place the airtight jar in the refrigerator for up to 5 days or freeze for up to 3 months. If frozen, thaw in the refrigerator. Before using, purée in a blender for about 30 seconds.

TIP: Make a sweet version! Begin with the raw cashews and water, then add 2 to 3 teaspoons maple syrup and 1 teaspoon flavored extract (vanilla, almond, or mint). Serve over sweet baked goods or fresh fruit or even in a hot breakfast bowl.

Per Serving (¼ cup): Calories: 192; Fat: 15g; Protein: 5g; Carbohydrates: 9g; Fiber: 2g; Sugar: 0g; Sodium: 252mg

BUFFALO-STYLE BARBECUE SAUCE

MAKES 2 CUPS

Prep: 10 minutes / Cook: 25 minutes

This isn't your traditional barbecue sauce! Some of the tang and smokiness is replaced with heat in this untraditional spin on a barbecue sauce that can be used on seitan, on tofu, or as a condiment on your favorite sandwich.

1 tablespoon vegetable oil or extra-virgin olive oil

½ cup chopped onion

1 teaspoon minced garlic (about 1 clove)

1 cup ketchup

½ cup hot sauce

¼ cup apple cider vinegar

1 tablespoon vegan Worcestershire sauce

Salt

1. In a medium saucepan over medium-low heat, heat the vegetable oil. Add the onion and garlic and cook for 5 minutes, stirring, until softened. Reduce the heat to low.

2. Add the ketchup, hot sauce, vinegar, and Worcestershire sauce. Season with salt, and stir. Cover and simmer for 20 minutes.

3. Pour into a mason jar or airtight container. Let cool before sealing the lid.

Storage: Place the airtight container in the refrigerator for up to 1 week.

TIP: This recipe can be made in an Instant Pot or other multicooker or pressure cooker. Add all the ingredients to the pot, cover, and cook on low pressure for 3 minutes. Use a quick release.

Per Serving (2 tablespoons): Calories: 26; Fat: 1g; Protein: 0g; Carbohydrates: 5g; Fiber: 0g; Sugar: 3g; Sodium: 290mg

SNACKS AND SWEETS

◀◀ Veggie Hummus Pinwheels (page 133)

RISOTTO BITES

Prep: 15 minutes / Cook: 20 minutes

I love repurposing leftovers! This is a great way to take a main dish and turn it into a snack with a completely different texture. Air-frying fans can follow the directions exactly but set the air fryer to 390°F and cook for about 7 minutes.

½ cup panko bread crumbs

1 teaspoon paprika

1 teaspoon chipotle powder or ground cayenne pepper

1½ cups cold Green Pea Risotto (page 69)

Nonstick cooking spray

1. Preheat the oven to 425°F. Line a baking sheet with parchment paper.

2. On a large plate, combine the panko, paprika, and chipotle powder. Set aside.

3. Roll 2 tablespoons of the risotto into a ball. Gently roll in the bread crumbs, and place on the prepared baking sheet. Repeat to make a total of 12 balls.

4. Spritz the tops of the risotto bites with nonstick cooking spray and bake for 15 to 20 minutes, until they begin to brown.

5. Cool completely before storing in a large airtight container in a single layer (add a piece of parchment paper for a second layer) or in a plastic freezer bag.

Storage: Place the airtight container in the refrigerator for up to 5 days or freeze for up to 2 months. To thaw, place in the refrigerator overnight. Microwave for 1½ to 3 minutes or reheat in a toaster oven set to 400°F for 5 to 10 minutes.

TIP: Instead of "bites," you can opt for veggie burgers! Use 1 cup cold risotto to form each patty.

Per Serving (6 bites): Calories: 100; Fat: 2g; Protein: 6g; Carbohydrates: 17g; Fiber: 5g; Sugar: 2g; Sodium: 165mg

KALE CHIPS

MAKES 2 SERVINGS

Prep: 5 minutes / Cook: 25 minutes, plus 15 minutes to cool

Perhaps the most stereotypically vegan recipe in this book, Kale Chips had to be done. I mean, what's better than turning an oh-so-good-for-you leafy green into a terrific alternative to greasy, bagged chips? I like to eat these up in two or three days. Perfect as a snack, they are also great crumbled over a salad for an alternative crouton or over soup to add a little texture.

1 large bunch kale

1 tablespoon extra-virgin olive oil

½ teaspoon chipotle powder

½ teaspoon smoked paprika

¼ teaspoon salt

1. Preheat the oven to 275°F. Line a large baking sheet with parchment paper.

2. In a large bowl, stem the kale and tear it into bite-size pieces. Add the olive oil, chipotle powder, smoked paprika, and salt. Toss the kale with tongs or your hands, coating each piece well.

3. Spread the kale over the parchment paper in a single layer. Bake for 25 minutes, turning halfway through, until crisp.

4. Cool for 10 to 15 minutes before dividing and storing in 2 airtight containers.

Storage: Store the airtight containers at room temperature for 2 to 3 days.

INGREDIENT TIP: If you prefer to limit oils, use unseasoned rice vinegar or balsamic vinegar as a substitute for the olive oil. You may not get the same level of crunch, but they're tasty all the same.

COOKING TIP: Leftover kale chips may not have the same crunch as when served hot out of the oven. If convenient, reheat in the oven (preheated to 400°F) for 5 to 10 minutes.

Per Serving: Calories: 144; Fat: 7g; Protein: 5g; Carbohydrates: 18g; Fiber: 3g; Sugar: 0g; Sodium: 363mg

TACO PITA PIZZAS

MAKES 4 SERVINGS

Prep: 5 minutes / Cook: 7 minutes

Mini pizzas are a terrific snack, and since we're using pita bread or Sandwich Thins, they actually reheat well! Notice that we aren't using vegan cheese? The refried beans add the creamy texture *and* a protein boost.

4 sandwich-size pita bread pieces or Sandwich Thins

1 cup vegetarian refried beans

1 cup pizza sauce

1 cup chopped mushrooms

1 teaspoon minced jalapeño (optional)

1. Preheat the oven to 400°F. Line a large baking sheet with parchment paper.

2. Assemble 4 pizzas: On each pita, spread about ¼ cup of refried beans. Pour ¼ cup of pizza sauce over the beans and spread evenly. Add ¼ cup of mushrooms. Sprinkle ¼ teaspoon of minced jalapeño (if using) over the mushrooms.

3. Place the pizzas on the prepared baking sheet and bake for 7 minutes.

4. Cool completely before placing each pizza in a freezer-safe plastic bag, or store together in one large airtight, freezer-safe container with parchment paper between the pizzas.

Storage: Place the pizzas in the freezer for up to 1 month. To defrost, refrigerate overnight. To reheat in a microwave, remove the pizza from the bag and place on a plate. Heat for 2 to 3 minutes. To reheat in a toaster oven, remove the pizza from the bag, place directly on the rack, and toast for 5 to 8 minutes at 400°F.

TIP: Most cans of refried beans equal 1½ cups. Save that remaining ½ cup to use as a bean dip with raw vegetables for a snack.

Per Serving: Calories: 148; Fat: 2g; Protein: 6g; Carbohydrates: 29g; Fiber: 5g; Sugar: 3g; Sodium: 492mg

SAVORY SEED CRACKERS

MAKES 20 CRACKERS

Prep: 5 minutes / Cook: 50 minutes

I created this recipe during a "raw vegan" phase (that lasted 10 days), and I really liked the crackers dehydrated. But I really love them baked! Try them with Edamame Hummus (page 118) or puréed Red Pepper Lentils (page 104).

¾ cup pumpkin seeds (pepitas)

½ cup sunflower seeds

½ cup sesame seeds

¼ cup chia seeds

1 teaspoon minced garlic (about 1 clove)

1 teaspoon tamari or soy sauce

1 teaspoon vegan Worcestershire sauce

½ teaspoon ground cayenne pepper

½ teaspoon dried oregano

½ cup water

1.   Preheat the oven to 325°F. Line a rimmed baking sheet with parchment paper.

2.   In a large bowl, combine the pumpkin seeds, sunflower seeds, sesame seeds, chia seeds, garlic, tamari, Worcestershire sauce, cayenne, oregano, and water. Transfer to the prepared baking sheet, spreading out to all sides.

3.   Bake for 25 minutes. Remove the pan from the oven, and flip the seed "dough" over so the wet side is up. Bake for another 20 to 25 minutes, until the sides are browned.

4.   Cool completely before breaking up into 20 pieces. Divide evenly among 4 glass jars and close tightly with lids.

Storage: Place the airtight jars on the counter or in the pantry for up to 2 weeks or freeze for up to 2 months. To thaw, set the containers out on a counter or in the pantry.

> **TIP:** Flaxseed can be a great addition, but remember that it must be ground. So simply add a tablespoon or two of ground flaxseed to the mix and a little extra water.

Per Serving (5 crackers): Calories: 339: Fat: 29g: Protein: 14g: Carbohydrates: 17g: Fiber: 8g: Sugar: 1g: Sodium: 96mg

TAMARI ALMONDS

MAKES 8 SERVINGS

Prep: 5 minutes / Cook: 15 minutes, plus 10 minutes to cool

I tend to pack nuts and seeds for afternoon snacks at the office or for a quick bite in the car on the way to a meeting. But after so many days, it can get a little boring. Elevate plain nuts with just a few ingredients, and you'll be inclined to use them as a snack *and* on salads, over a hot bowl of beans and grains, and even chopped over vegan ice cream.

1 pound raw almonds

3 tablespoons tamari or soy sauce

2 tablespoons extra-virgin olive oil

1 tablespoon nutritional yeast

1 to 2 teaspoons chili powder, to taste

1. Preheat the oven to 400°F. Line a baking sheet with parchment paper.

2. In a medium bowl, combine the almonds, tamari, and olive oil until well coated. Spread the almonds on the prepared baking sheet and roast for 10 to 15 minutes, until browned.

3. Cool for 10 minutes, then season with the nutritional yeast and chili powder.

4. Transfer to a glass jar and close tightly with a lid.

Storage: Store at room temperature for up to 5 days, in the refrigerator for 2 weeks, or in the freezer for up to 4 months.

TIP: Because these freeze so well, consider doubling the recipe and filling several jars for the freezer. Reheat in the microwave for 2 to 3 minutes or crisp up in an air fryer on 390°F for 5 to 8 minutes.

Per Serving: Calories: 364; Fat: 32g; Protein: 13g; Carbohydrates: 13g; Fiber: 7g; Sugar: 3g; Sodium: 381mg

ROASTED CHICKPEAS

MAKES 4 SERVINGS

Prep: 5 minutes / Cook: 30 minutes

Uber-vegan, roasted chickpeas are a protein-rich snack. In this recipe I'm using spices that we've set up for your meal prep pantry, but remember that you can substitute 2 teaspoons of spices of your choice (try ground ginger and cinnamon and opt for maple syrup instead of the olive oil).

1 (14.5-ounce) can chickpeas, drained but not rinsed

1 teaspoon extra-virgin olive oil or 2 teaspoons reserved chickpea brine (aquafaba)

1 teaspoon smoked paprika

1 teaspoon garlic powder

1. Preheat the oven to 425°F. Line a baking sheet with parchment paper.

2. After draining the chickpeas (reserving the brine if using the aquafaba as an oil replacement), pat dry with a paper towel. Transfer to a medium bowl. Add the olive oil, paprika, and garlic powder. Using a wooden spoon or your hands, toss gently to coat.

3. Spread the chickpeas out on the prepared baking sheet in a single layer. Roast for 30 minutes, rotating the baking sheet after 15 minutes.

4. Turn the oven off, open the oven door about five inches, and allow the chickpeas to cool in the oven. Transfer all of the chickpeas into a glass pint jar or divide evenly among 4 (4-ounce) jelly jars. Cool completely before closing tightly with lids.

Storage: Store at room temperature for up to 3 days.

> **TIP:** Crispy out of the oven, the texture will change a bit after a day or two. Add them to salads or as a topping to a bowl of grains and greens for an alternative to a snack. Or place them in a bowl and reheat in a toaster oven heated to 425°F for 10 minutes to "spruce" them up.

Per Serving: Calories: 157; Fat: 3g; Protein: 6g; Carbohydrates: 28g; Fiber: 6g; Sugar: 0g; Sodium: 359mg

BAKED POTATO CHIPS

MAKES 4 SERVINGS

Prep: 10 minutes, plus 20 minutes to soak / Cook: 30 minutes

A nod to the barbecue potato chip, these wholesome baked potato slices are great as a snack, as a side dish, or even chopped or shredded and served over soups and salads.

1 large Russet potato

1 teaspoon paprika

½ teaspoon garlic salt

¼ teaspoon vegan sugar

¼ teaspoon onion powder

¼ teaspoon chipotle powder or chili powder

⅛ teaspoon salt

⅛ teaspoon ground mustard

⅛ teaspoon ground cayenne pepper

1 teaspoon canola oil

⅛ teaspoon liquid smoke

1. Wash and peel the potato. Cut into thin, $\frac{1}{10}$-inch slices (a mandoline slicer or the slicer blade in a food processor is helpful for consistently sized slices).

2. Fill a large bowl with enough very cold water to cover the potato. Transfer the potato slices to the bowl and soak for 20 minutes.

3. Preheat the oven to 400°F. Line a baking sheet with parchment paper.

4. In a small bowl, combine the paprika, garlic salt, sugar, onion powder, chipotle powder, salt, mustard, and cayenne.

5. Drain and rinse the potato slices and pat dry with a paper towel. Transfer to a large bowl. Add the canola oil, liquid smoke, and spice mixture to the bowl. Toss to coat. Transfer the potatoes to the prepared baking sheet. Bake for 15 minutes. Flip the chips over and bake for 15 minutes longer, until browned.

6. Transfer the chips to 4 storage containers or large glass jars. Let cool before closing the lids tightly.

Storage: Store on the countertop or in the pantry for up to 3 days.

TIP: Each day the chips will lose a little bit of their crunch. This isn't a bad thing; I just want to manage expectations. On day 2, consider using them as a crouton for a salad, and on day 3, shred them and serve over "Beefy" Bean Chili (page 78).

Per Serving: Calories: 89; Fat: 1g; Protein: 2g; Carbohydrates: 18g; Fiber: 2g; Sugar: 1g; Sodium: 65mg

VEGGIE HUMMUS PINWHEELS

| MAKES 3 SERVINGS

Prep: 10 minutes

These cute little bites are a great way to get in your beans, greens, and grains finger food–style. We're making only enough for three meal prep snacks because though easy, fast, and fun to eat, stuffed tortillas need to be consumed within 3 days for everything to taste fresh.

3 whole-grain, spinach, flour, or gluten-free tortillas

3 large Swiss chard leaves

¾ cup Edamame Hummus (page 118) or prepared hummus

¾ cup shredded carrots

1.   Lay 1 tortilla flat on a cutting board. Place 1 Swiss chard leaf over the tortilla. Spread ¼ cup of hummus over the Swiss chard. Spread ¼ cup of carrots over the hummus.

2.   Starting at one end of the tortilla, roll tightly toward the opposite side. Slice each roll up into 6 pieces. Place in a single-serving storage container. Repeat with the remaining tortillas and filling and seal the lids.

Storage: Place the airtight containers in the refrigerator for up to 3 days.

> **TIP:** Store these pinwheel pieces in a container with extra room. You can turn this snack into a meal simply by adding fresh-cut raw vegetables and fruit to the container for a healthy, well-balanced finger-food lunch or dinner.

Per Serving: Calories: 254; Fat: 8g; Protein: 10g; Carbohydrates: 39g; Fiber: 8g; Sugar: 4g; Sodium: 488mg

BAKED GRANOLA

MAKES 6 SERVINGS

Prep: 10 minutes / Cook: 30 minutes

This is a snack and so much more! It's super easy and uses many basic pantry staples: oats, dried fruit, nuts, and seeds. As important, you can easily double this recipe, and it can be used as a snack, as cereal for breakfast, or as a topping for ice cream.

3 cups rolled oats

1 cup unsweetened dried fruit (cherries, apricots, raisins)

½ cup chopped nuts (walnuts, pecans, cashews)

¼ cup pumpkin seeds (pepitas)

2 tablespoons sesame seeds

¼ cup maple syrup or agave syrup

2 tablespoons coconut oil or extra-virgin olive oil

½ teaspoon salt (optional)

1. Preheat the oven to 300°F. Line a baking sheet with parchment paper.

2. In a large bowl, combine the oats, fruit, nuts, pumpkin seeds, sesame seeds, maple syrup, coconut oil, and salt (if using). Toss well to coat.

3. Pour the granola onto the prepared baking sheet and spread out evenly with a spatula or your hands. Bake for 25 to 30 minutes, stirring about halfway through, until golden and lightly toasted.

4. Transfer to a large mason jar or 6 single-serving storage containers. Close tightly with lids.

Storage: Store the airtight jars in a cool, dry place or refrigerate for up to 2 weeks.

TIP: Try using this granola in the Smoothie Breakfast Bowl (page 60).

Per Serving: Calories: 367; Fat: 13g; Protein: 8g; Carbohydrates: 58g; Fiber: 6g; Sugar: 23g; Sodium: 8mg

BANANA-NUT BREAD BARS

MAKES 9 BARS

Prep: 5 minutes / Cook: 30 minutes

This banana "bread" stars oats, instead of flour, making it another wholesome nod to what's likely an old recipe favorite.

Nonstick cooking spray (optional)

2 large ripe bananas

1 tablespoon maple syrup

½ teaspoon vanilla extract

2 cups old-fashioned rolled oats

½ teaspoons salt

¼ cup chopped walnuts

1. Preheat the oven to 350°F. Lightly coat a 9-by-9-inch baking pan with nonstick cooking spray (if using) or line with parchment paper for oil-free baking.

2. In a medium bowl, mash the bananas with a fork. Add the maple syrup and vanilla extract and mix well. Add the oats, salt, and walnuts, mixing well.

3. Transfer the batter to the baking pan and bake for 25 to 30 minutes, until the top is crispy.

4. Cool completely before slicing into 9 bars. Transfer to an airtight storage container or a large plastic bag.

Storage: Store at room temperature for up to 5 days. To freeze, place in a large plastic freezer bag for up to 4 months.

TIP: Great as a snack, these are equally perfect for breakfast!

Per Serving (1 bar): Calories: 73; Fat: 1g; Protein: 2g; Carbohydrates: 15g; Fiber: 2g; Sugar: 5g; Sodium: 129mg

CASHEW-CHOCOLATE TRUFFLES

MAKES 12 TRUFFLES

Prep: 15 minutes, plus 1 hour to set

These "truffles" are so wholesome, you could easily eat them for breakfast (I crumble one over a hot bowl of oatmeal). They are excellent as a midday or late-night snack, too.

1 cup raw cashews, soaked in water overnight

¾ cup pitted dates

2 tablespoons coconut oil

1 cup unsweetened shredded coconut, divided

1 to 2 tablespoons cocoa powder, to taste

1. In a food processor, combine the cashews, dates, coconut oil, ½ cup of shredded coconut, and cocoa powder. Pulse until fully incorporated; it will resemble chunky cookie dough.

2. Spread the remaining ½ cup of shredded coconut on a plate.

3. Form the mixture into tablespoon-size balls and roll on the plate to cover with the shredded coconut. Transfer to a parchment paper–lined plate or baking sheet. Repeat to make 12 truffles. Place the truffles in the refrigerator for 1 hour to set.

4. Transfer the truffles to a storage container or freezer-safe bag and seal.

Storage: Place the airtight container in the refrigerator for 1 week to 10 days or freeze for up to 3 months. To thaw, refrigerate overnight. Eat cold or at room temperature.

TIP: These truffles are great to fuel a workout. They fit easily into a backpack for a hike or into a bike jersey for a long ride.

Per Serving (1 truffle): Calories 238: Fat: 18g; Protein: 3g; Carbohydrates: 16g; Fiber: 4g; Sugar: 9g; Sodium: 9mg

MINTY FRUIT SALAD

MAKES 4 SERVINGS

Prep: 10 minutes

This is the kind of dish you could set out at a dinner party to impress, but we both know it's incredibly simple. If your local store carries cut pineapple, you're going to be able to whip this up in 5 minutes.

¼ cup lemon juice (about 2 small lemons)

4 teaspoons maple syrup or agave syrup

2 cups chopped pineapple

2 cups chopped strawberries

2 cups raspberries

1 cup blueberries

8 fresh mint leaves

Beginning with 1 mason jar, add the ingredients in this order: 1 tablespoon of lemon juice, 1 teaspoon of maple syrup, ½ cup of pineapple, ½ cup of strawberries, ½ cup of raspberries, ¼ cup of blueberries, and 2 mint leaves. Repeat to fill 3 more jars. Close the jars tightly with lids.

Storage: Place the airtight jars in the refrigerator for up to 3 days.

TIP: To turn this fruit snack into a meal, start with ½ cup plain vegan yogurt in the jar, assemble as directed, and finish with ¼ cup Baked Granola (page 134) or slivered almonds.

Per Serving: Calories: 138; Fat: 1g; Protein: 2g; Carbohydrates: 34g; Fiber: 8g; Sugar: 22g; Sodium: 6mg

Measurement Conversions

Volume Equivalents (Liquid)

US STANDARD	US STANDARD (OUNCES)	METRIC (APPROXIMATE)
2 TABLESPOONS	1 FL. OZ.	30 ML
¼ CUP	2 FL. OZ.	60 ML
½ CUP	4 FL. OZ.	120 ML
1 CUP	8 FL. OZ.	240 ML
1½ CUPS	12 FL. OZ.	355 ML
2 CUPS OR 1 PINT	16 FL. OZ.	475 ML
4 CUPS OR 1 QUART	32 FL. OZ.	1 L
1 GALLON	128 FL. OZ.	4 L

Oven Temperatures

FAHRENHEIT (F)	CELSIUS (C) (APPROXIMATE)
250°F	120°C
300°F	150°C
325°F	165°C
350°F	180°C
375°F	190°C
400°F	200°C
425°F	220°C
450°F	230°C

Volume Equivalents (Dry)

US STANDARD	METRIC (APPROXIMATE)
⅛ TEASPOON	0.5 ML
¼ TEASPOON	1 ML
½ TEASPOON	2 ML
¾ TEASPOON	4 ML
1 TEASPOON	5 ML
1 TABLESPOON	15 ML
¼ CUP	59 ML
⅓ CUP	79 ML
½ CUP	118 ML
⅔ CUP	156 ML
¾ CUP	177 ML
1 CUP	235 ML
2 CUPS OR 1 PINT	475 ML
3 CUPS	700 ML
4 CUPS OR 1 QUART	1 L
½ GALLON	2 L
1 GALLON	4 L

Weight Equivalents

US STANDARD	METRIC (APPROXIMATE)
½ OUNCE	15 GRAMS
1 OUNCE	30 GRAMS
2 OUNCES	60 GRAMS
4 OUNCES	115 GRAMS
8 OUNCES	225 GRAMS
12 OUNCES	340 GRAMS
16 OUNCES OR 1 POUND	455 GRAMS

Recipe Index

RECIPE TITLE	GLUTEN-FREE	NUT-FREE	OIL-FREE
Asian-Inspired Chili, 84	X	X	X
Baked Brussels Sprouts, 98	X	X	
Baked Granola, 134	X		
Baked Potato Chips, 132	X	X	
Baked Wild Rice, 111	X		X
Balsamic Black Beans, 105	X	X	X
Banana-Nut Bread Bars, 135	X		X
Barley Breakfast Bowl, 57		X	X
Basic Baked Potato, 99	X	X	X
"Beefy" Bean Chili, 78	X	X	X
Buffalo-Style Barbecue Sauce, 123	X	X	
Caesar-Style Dressing, 117	X	X	
Cajun Sweet Potatoes, 91	X	X	
Caramelized Onion and Beet Salad, 96	X	X	X
Cashew-Chocolate Truffles, 136	X		
Cashew Cream, 122	X		
Cheesy Mushroom Polenta, 76	X	X	
Chickpea and Artichoke Curry, 87	X	X	X

RECIPE TITLE	GLUTEN-FREE	NUT-FREE	OIL-FREE
Cinnamon and Spice Overnight Oats, 56	X		X
Cowboy Caviar Salad, 80	X	X	X
Cucumber and Onion Quinoa Salad, 85	X	X	
Curried Peanut Butter, 116	X		
Dilly White Beans, 106	X	X	X
Easy Kitchari, 82–83	X	X	X
Easy Marinara, 121	X	X	X
Edamame Hummus, 118	X	X	X
Five-Spice Farro, 108		X	X
Garlic and Herb Zoodles, 93	X	X	
Great Green Smoothie, 59	X	X	X
Green Pea Risotto, 69	X	X	
Healthy Mac 'n' Cheese, 86	X	X	X
Italian Lentils, 103	X	X	X
Kale Chips, 127	X	X	X
Mashed Potatoes and Kale with White Beans, 70–71	X	X	X
Mediterranean Beans with Greens, 75	X	X	X
Minty Fruit Salad, 137	X	X	X
Miso Root Veggies, 95	X	X	X
Miso Spaghetti Squash, 92	X	X	X

RECIPE TITLE	GLUTEN-FREE	NUT-FREE	OIL-FREE
Not-Tuna Salad, 73	X	X	
Parm-y Kale Pesto, 114	X		
Peppered Pinto Beans, 102	X	X	X
Pesto Pearled Barley, 109			
Pumpkin Steel-Cut Oats, 54	X	X	X
Quinoa and Kale Bowl, 81	X	X	X
Quinoa Pilaf, 79	X		X
Red Bean and Corn Salad, 74	X		
Red Pepper Lentils, 104	X	X	X
Risotto Bites, 126		X	
Roasted Chickpeas, 131	X	X	X
Savory Oatmeal Porridge, 55			X
Savory Pancakes, 64–65		X	
Savory Seed Crackers, 129	X	X	X
Smoky Coleslaw, 94	X	X	
Smoothie Breakfast Bowl, 60	X		
Spanish Rice, 110	X	X	X
Spicy Fruit and Veggie Gazpacho, 97	X	X	X
Steamed Cauliflower, 90	X	X	X
Sushi-Style Quinoa, 107	X	X	X
Sweet Potato and Black Bean Hash, 58	X	X	X
Sweet Tamari Tempeh with Roasted Vegetables, 68	X	X	X

RECIPE TITLE	GLUTEN-FREE	NUT-FREE	OIL-FREE
Taco Pita Pizzas, 128		X	
Tamari Almonds, 130	X		
TLT Wrap, 77	X	X	
Tofu-Spinach Scramble, 62–63	X	X	X
Tortilla Breakfast Casserole, 61	X	X	
Vegan Thousand Island, 119	X	X	X
Veggie Hummus Pinwheels, 133	X	X	X
Warm Vegetable "Salad," 72	X		X
White Bean and Sun-dried Tomato Dip, 115	X	X	
White Bean Gravy, 120	X	X	

Index

Acknowledgments

Heartfelt thanks to Elizabeth Castoria for entrusting me with a book project that speaks to the core of my approach to teaching others how easy and delicious vegan eating can be. And more kudos for the Callisto Media team: my editor Stacy Wagner-Kinnear who actually made the editing process fun (I mean it!), and Nell McPherson and Erum Khan for taking such care while combing the fine details.

I am immensely grateful to Epicentral Coworking in Colorado Springs. It's not just a place I "office." It's a community and my community of entrepreneurs and content creators support me daily (and they let me test recipes on them!). Epicentral is also the home of my Colorado Springs Vegan Cooking Academy because Lisa Tessarowicz, Frank Frey, and Kayla Battles are all about collaboration.

Ginny Messina and Victoria Moran, thank you for believing in me, creating with me, and for grounding me in why I do this work: for the animals.

Mom and Dad, everything I have accomplished is because you've always told me I could.

And last, but never least, my heart swells with gratitude for my husband Dave. Because of his unwavering support I get to create and recreate who I am, what I stand for, and how I choose to live and love in the world. And with whom I have the privilege of "co-parenting" our furry companions Oliver and Harry.

About the Author

JL Fields is the founder and culinary director of the Colorado Springs Vegan Cooking Academy. She is a Master Vegan Lifestyle Coach and Educator, Food for Life instructor, chef instructor in the culinary program at the University of New Mexico–Taos, personal chef, career coach, and corporate consultant. JL is the producer and host of the cooking show *Real World Vegan Cooking* and the radio program *Easy Vegan*. She writes the monthly vegan dining review for the Colorado Springs *Gazette*.

JL is the author of the revised and updated *Vegan Pressure Cooking: More Than 100 Delicious Grain, Bean, and One-Pot Meals Using a Traditional or Electric Pressure Cooker or Instant Pot* and *The Vegan Air Fryer: The Healthier Way to Enjoy Deep-Fried Flavors*, as well as the coauthor of *The Main Street Vegan Academy Cookbook: Over 100 Plant-Sourced Recipes Plus Practical Tips for the Healthiest, Most Compassionate You* and *Vegan for Her: The Woman's Guide to Being Healthy and Fit on a Plant-Based Diet*. She lives in Colorado Springs with her husband Dave, their feline rescue Oliver, and canine rescue Harry.